Name:

_____

Start Date:

_____

End Date:

_____

refreshed

MEETING WITH JESUS

BECOMING LOVE IN ACTION

Cleere Cherry Reaves

DEVOTIONAL GUIDE

Introduction

Have you found yourself using the terms "exhausted," "busy," "stressed," or "drained"? Due to our fast-paced, innovative yet often demanding world, and our own personal tendencies, many of us have constructed a new normal that operates from this place of constant exhaustion rather than fulfillment. However, our heavenly Father and the Shepherd of our souls has much different hopes for our lives. What would it look like to live from a refreshed place? What would change if we let rest become our posture, hope determine our perspective, and reliance on the Father our strength? What if we became love in action?

This study will dig into different passages and stories from Scripture, allowing us to get a firsthand look at the person of love Himself as He worked miracles with His own hands and through the hands of His people. As we witness real love in action, we will learn to be more and more like Jesus. And isn't that why we are here? Is there a greater dream, a more important commitment, or a higher calling than that?

So, join me in this thirty-day study and let your heart be both encouraged and challenged as you read and reflect on God's Word. Isn't it a beautiful thing that we have the authority to change our rhythm, show up differently, and live from a place of abundance? So, gather your friends, or just grab a pen. Either way, I believe we will grasp a greater understanding of the "more" life that you and I are after. I know that He will meet us right where we are and refresh our weary souls.

If you'd like to receive daily refreshment, you can find me on Instagram at @cleerelystated, listen to my podcast, "Let's Be Cleere," or find all my products at www.cleerelystated.com.

I am proud of you for being here.
Now, let's get started.

Xoxo,

Cleere

Contents

How do I use this devotional guide?

I love this devotional guide because it encourages you to experience the life-changing message of God's Word for yourself. *Each of the thirty entries includes the following:*

LEARN ABOUT HIS LOVE

Each entry starts with Scripture passages that address the topic of God's love. God's Word reveals how His great love for us enables us to love and care for others. Be sure to read each verse, say the words out loud, and maybe even memorize these verses so you can recite them in times of need.

LOVE OUT LOUD

Here is where I lay it all out for you—my heart. I mean it when I say that this devotional guide challenged me on a personal level. I started asking myself, "Am I loving correctly? Or am I judgmental? Do I really, without a doubt, believe that God loves me completely?" You'll see a message from me in every entry under the subhead "Love Out Loud." This is where I wrestle with my actions and thoughts on a personal level. Welcome to my journey! I hope you're inspired to dive deep with me.

PONDER HIS LOVE

Your turn! It's time to answer a few questions about where you are, how you're feeling, and who you are becoming. Sometimes the answers will come quickly, and sometimes you may have to do some soul searching, but either way, the exercise of writing it down will help you acknowledge and focus on where you are on your spiritual journey. Be honest! This is your safe place.

COMMUNICATE WITH LOVE

Let's talk to our Creator about it! Friends, I cannot stress it enough—we can memorize the Scriptures, work hard to follow all the rules, and know just what to say at just the right times, but if we aren't talking to Jesus about it, we're missing the whole point! Take time to lift it all up to God and feel the weight melt off your shoulders.

Want to dive in a little more? Here is a list of Scripture passages for you to study. The Bible is the greatest love story ever written. I invite you to look up the additional Scriptures and ask God to reveal His heart to you in new, amazing ways.

QR Codes

I created some videos for you—you can find them by scanning the QR codes found in the Introduction, and then after every six entries. All you need to do is scan the QR code at the bottom of each entry and the videos will pop up. Here's how to open a QR code:

1. Open the camera on your phone.

2. Point the camera at the QR code (the small square barcode-looking, black-and-white box in the bottom right corner). If your front-facing camera is on, first tap the camera-shaped icon to flip it.

3. Make sure the QR code is centered on the camera screen. All four edges of the QR code should be on the screen.

4. Wait for the code to scan. (It should scan almost immediately.)

5. Open the QR code's content. Tap the notification that appears at the top of the screen to open the QR code's webpage or other information.

It's my hope that through the pages in this devotional guide, your soul will be refreshed in a way that those around you will be forever transformed by the love that is radiating off of you. Are you ready?

Let's get started!

LEARN ABOUT HIS LOVE

Empowered to Act

MATTHEW 14:13–36 NLT

As soon as Jesus heard the news, He left in a boat to a remote area to be alone. But the crowds heard where He was headed and followed on foot from many towns. Jesus saw the huge crowd as He stepped from the boat, and He had compassion on them and healed their sick.

That evening the disciples came to Him and said, "This is a remote place, and it's already getting late. Send the crowds away so they can go to the villages and buy food for themselves."

But Jesus said, "That isn't necessary—you feed them."

"But we have only five loaves of bread and two fish!" they answered.

"Bring them here," He said. Then He told the people to sit down on the grass. Jesus took the five loaves and two fish, looked up toward heaven, and blessed them. Then, breaking the loaves into pieces, He gave the bread to the disciples, who distributed it to the people. They all ate as much as they wanted, and afterward, the disciples picked up twelve baskets of leftovers. About 5,000 men were fed that day, in addition to all the women and children!

JESUS WALKS ON WATER

Immediately after this, Jesus insisted that His disciples get back into the boat and cross to the other side of the lake, while He sent the people home. After sending them home, He went up into the hills by Himself to pray. Night fell while He was there alone.

Meanwhile, the disciples were in trouble far away from land, for a strong wind had risen, and they were fighting heavy waves. About three o'clock in the morning Jesus came toward them, walking on the water. When the disciples saw Him walking on the water, they were terrified. In their fear, they cried out, "It's a ghost!"

But Jesus spoke to them at once. "Don't be afraid," He said. "Take courage. I am here!"

Then Peter called to Him, "Lord, if it's really You, tell me to come to You, walking on the water."

"Yes, come," Jesus said.

So Peter went over the side of the boat and walked on the water toward Jesus. But when he saw the strong wind and the waves, he was terrified and began to sink. "Save me, Lord!" he shouted.

Jesus immediately reached out and grabbed him. "You have so little faith," Jesus said. "Why did you doubt Me?"

When they climbed back into the boat, the wind stopped. Then the disciples worshiped Him. "You really are the Son of God!" they exclaimed.

After they had crossed the lake, they landed at Gennesaret. When the people recognized Jesus, the news of His arrival spread quickly throughout the whole area, and soon people were bringing all their sick to be healed. They begged Him to let the sick touch at least the fringe of His robe, and all who touched Him were healed.

Reading over these verses, I am amazed at the ways Jesus responds to His people. While Jesus is full of compassion, He is also committed to helping His disciples realize the authority that they have as His followers. We see that when the people of the crowd were hungry, Jesus says, "That isn't necessary—you feed them." Then again, when Peter is walking on the water toward Jesus and takes his focus off of Him, Jesus responds with, "You have so little faith. Why did you doubt Me?" I love that Jesus was unapologetic about the need for His followers to take up their shield of faith and realize the assignment in front of them.

This brought many instances to my mind, in particular in my career, when Jesus intervened and redirected my eyes to ask me, "Haven't I already given You what You need? Offer that." Many times, like the little boy and the disciples, I felt as though what I had to give was simply not enough. Or, I would step out in courage and lose my focus on the water, immediately calling for His rescue. In typical Jesus fashion, He continually reminds me of His presence and His provision. Because He is our Father, He knows that if He just does everything for us without our getting involved, we will miss out on becoming like Him, and isn't that the point?

Now, when my supply feels like not enough, I try to remind myself that the miracle is found in the multiplication of what I already have. And when fear begins to kick in, I recheck my focus. Jesus has empowered me to act, ensuring my faith has the ability to come alive.

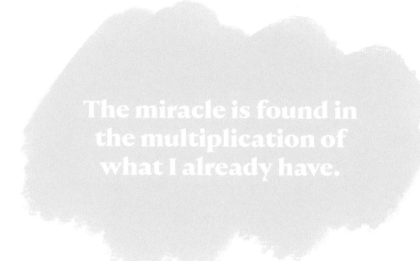

The miracle is found in
the multiplication of
what I already have.

PONDER HIS LOVE

1. *Jesus performed the miracle of the bread and the fish, showing His provision. Immediately after, the disciples went on the boat and doubted His provision. How do you see this tendency in your own life—witnessing His provision and immediately being placed in a position to doubt it or trust it?*

2. *The story of Jesus feeding the five thousand mentions they had leftovers. Why do you think Jesus made sure to include this in the story?*

3. When Peter was walking on the water, it was only when his eyes were taken off Jesus that he began to sink. What in your own life most easily distracts you from Jesus?

4. When the disciples saw Jesus walking on the water, they didn't recognize Him because they didn't plan for Him to be there. When have you noticed in your own life how quickly you begin to doubt Jesus and not recognize Him when you aren't prepared for His presence?

5. Is there a particular situation or circumstance in which Jesus is asking you to take courage and walk on the water in your own life? If so, what is holding you back?

Dear Lord, thank You for this miracle story that gives us such a beautiful glimpse of the nearness and empowerment You give Your people. Much like the disciples, I often look at my situations and wonder how the provision will come as my fear tries to take the microphone. In these moments, I sometimes question if You see me or know what I need. But then I remember that the space between what I see and what is needed is the margin for my faith to come alive.

Would You broaden my perspective and heighten my awareness of what to do, how to respond, and when to leap? When my focus is taken off of You, my circumstances overwhelm my soul; but when I remember Your presence and the promises You make in Your Word, I find peace and rest again. Help me be a person of action, not just intention. Show me how to recognize the assignment in the midst of the hurried pace of this world. I know when I make myself available, You will do all that I cannot.

Thank You for giving me opportunities to activate my faith. You can't multiply what I don't give. Today, I surrender all that I have, lay it at Your feet, and anchor myself in Your presence. The pressure is off my shoulders and on Yours. Leaning into You, my supply is abundantly renewed and my strength is secure.

In the faithful and empowering name of Jesus, amen.

MEDITATE ON HIS LOVE

DEUTERONOMY 31:6 ESV

Be strong and courageous. Do not fear or be in dread of them, for it is the Lord your God who goes with you. He will not leave you or forsake you.

II PETER 1:3–4 ESV

His divine power has granted to us all things that pertain to life and godliness, through the knowledge of him who called us to his own glory and excellence, by which he has granted to us his precious and very great promises, so that through them you may become partakers of the divine nature, having escaped from the corruption that is in the world because of sinful desire.

I TIMOTHY 4:12 ESV

Let no one despise you for your youth, but set the believers an example in speech, in conduct, in love, in faith, in purity.

EPHESIANS 3:16 ESV

That according to the riches of his glory he may grant you to be strengthened with power through his Spirit in your inner being.

ACTS 1:8 ESV

You will receive power when the Holy Spirit has come upon you, and you will be my witnesses in Jerusalem and in all Judea and Samaria, and to the end of the earth.

LEARN ABOUT HIS LOVE

Healed through Faith

Peter and John went to the Temple one afternoon to take part in the three o'clock prayer service. As they approached the Temple, a man lame from birth was being carried in. Each day he was put beside the Temple gate, the one called the Beautiful Gate, so he could beg from the people going into the Temple. When he saw Peter and John about to enter, he asked them for some money.

Peter and John looked at him intently, and Peter said, "Look at us!" The lame man looked at them eagerly, expecting some money. But Peter said, "I don't have any silver or gold for you. But I'll give you what I have. In the name of Jesus Christ the Nazarene, get up and walk!"

Then Peter took the lame man by the right hand and helped him up. And as he did, the man's feet and ankles were instantly healed and strengthened. He jumped up, stood on his feet, and began to walk! Then, walking, leaping, and praising God, he went into the Temple with them.

All the people saw him walking and heard him praising God. When they realized he was the lame beggar they had seen so often at the Beautiful Gate, they were absolutely astounded! They all rushed out in amazement to Solomon's Colonnade, where the man was holding tightly to Peter and John.

PETER PREACHES IN THE TEMPLE

Peter saw his opportunity and addressed the crowd. "People of Israel," he said, "what is so surprising about this? And why stare at us as though we had made this man walk by our own power or godliness? For it is the God of Abraham, Isaac, and Jacob—the God of all our ancestors—who has brought glory to His servant Jesus by doing this. This is the same Jesus whom you handed over and rejected before Pilate, despite Pilate's decision to release Him. You rejected this holy, righteous One and instead demanded the release of a murderer. You killed the Author of life, but God raised Him from the dead. And we are witnesses of this fact!

"Through faith in the name of Jesus, this man was healed—and you know how crippled he was before. Faith in Jesus' name has healed him before your very eyes.

"Friends, I realize that what you and your leaders did to Jesus was done in ignorance. But God was fulfilling what all the prophets had foretold about the Messiah—that He must suffer these things. Now repent of your sins and turn to God, so that your sins may be wiped away. Then times of refreshment will come from the presence of the Lord, and He will again send you Jesus, your appointed Messiah. For He must remain in heaven until the time for the final restoration of all things, as God promised long ago through His holy prophets. Moses said, 'The LORD your God will raise up for you a Prophet like me from among your own people. Listen carefully to everything He tells you.' Then Moses said, 'Anyone who will not listen to that Prophet will be completely cut off from God's people.'

"Starting with Samuel, every prophet spoke about what is happening today. You are the children of those prophets, and you are included in the covenant God promised to your ancestors. For God said to Abraham, 'Through your descendants all the families on earth will be blessed.' When God raised up His servant, Jesus, He sent Him first to you people of Israel, to bless you by turning each of you back from your sinful ways."

PETER AND JOHN BEFORE THE COUNCIL

While Peter and John were speaking to the people, they were confronted by the priests, the captain of the Temple guard, and some of the Sadducees. These leaders were very disturbed that Peter and John were teaching the people that through Jesus there is a resurrection of the dead. They arrested them and, since it was already evening, put them in jail until morning. But many of the people who heard their message believed it, so the number of men who believed now totaled about 5,000.

The next day the council of all the rulers and elders and teachers of religious law met in Jerusalem. Annas the high priest was there, along with Caiaphas, John, Alexander, and other relatives of the high priest. They brought in the two disciples and demanded, "By what power, or in whose name, have you done this?"

Then Peter, filled with the Holy Spirit, said to them, "Rulers and elders of our people, are we being questioned today because we've done a good deed for a crippled man? Do you want to know how he was healed? Let me clearly state to all of you and to all the people of Israel that he was healed by the powerful name of Jesus Christ the Nazarene, the man you crucified but whom God raised from the dead."

I think we all need to pause for just a moment and really recognize the boldness of these two disciples, Peter and John. They were headed to a regular prayer service at church when they noticed the lame beggar on the side of the road. Instead of walking away because they didn't have the riches he longed for, Peter and John boldly intervened, knowing that what they did have to offer—the healing of Jesus Christ—was far better. Then, once religious officials realized what had happened, they were determined to punish the men for being so bold.

There was no obligation for Peter and John to stop, nor for them to continue preaching. They simply believed that God was who He said He was, and if that was the case, how could they have true compassion for the lame beggar and these village people and not speak about the Great Healer and Deliverer?

This story challenges my spirit and confronts my fears. Even though I know that Scripture tells us we will face rejection and consequences from the world for standing up for our faith, I still find myself tempted to seek the affirmation from those around me. If others don't agree, do I grow weary in spirit or silent in voice? Am I worried that when I do show up, God might abandon me?

Because of Peter and John, over five thousand more friends will be in heaven. Let us take a lesson from them—we will never regret speaking for Jesus. There is freedom in letting our light shine.

There is freedom in
letting our light shine.

1. *This passage says that Peter and John were on their way to an everyday prayer service when they performed this miracle. Do you find yourself becoming numb to the people around you amidst your normal routines and everyday schedule?*

2. *When Peter extended his hand, do you think he was nervous to see if the miracle would actually happen? When is a time you've been nervous because you worried that God might not come through? How did you handle it?*

3. *We see that Peter and John immediately faced opposition after the miracle took place. Have you ever faced backlash after a breakthrough?*

4. *Where in your life do you believe Jesus is asking you to be more bold? What would that require you to do or say?*

5. *Think about someone in your life who operates in boldness and courage. How have you seen it change lives or alter circumstances?*

Dear Lord, thank You for the gift of this story about Peter and John and reminding me that these were two ordinary men. However, their extraordinary faith in You allowed them to have supernatural vision and courage in an otherwise ordinary situation.

Father, I want to be more like that. Will You help me be as bold as a lion and as gentle as a dove? In all that I do, say, and give, I want to reflect the strength and truth of Your Word. I never have to fear that You will abandon me, or second-guess Your ownership over my life.

When opposition strikes, help it not surprise me. You have already told me that I will face trouble here! It's why You came. But Jesus, You aren't worried or shocked by this; You simply desire that I lock eyes with You, cling to truth, and let it be the loudest voice in my life.

In the conversations I have, help me boldly speak life and refuse to let gossip have a place.

In unexpected circumstances, show me how to walk forward with boldness when I don't always understand or know what's next.

In the everyday situations and mundane moments of my life, guide me in extending bold compassion, offering bold generosity, and giving bold love.

In Jesus' name, amen.

MEDITATE ON HIS LOVE

PROVERBS 28:1 NIV

The wicked flee though no one pursues, but the righteous are as bold as a lion.

HEBREWS 13:6 NLT

So we can say with confidence, "The LORD is my helper, so I will have no fear. What can mere people do to me?"

ACTS 4:28–29 NLT

But everything they did was determined beforehand according to Your will. And now, O Lord, hear their threats, and give us, Your servants, great boldness in preaching Your word.

ACTS 4:13 NLT

The members of the council were amazed when they saw the boldness of Peter and John, for they could see that they were ordinary men with no special training in the Scriptures. They also recognized them as men who had been with Jesus.

JOHN 14:12 ESV

Truly, truly, I say to you, whoever believes in me will also do the works that I do; and greater works than these will he do, because I am going to the Father.

LEARN ABOUT HIS LOVE

Moved by Compassion

MATTHEW 25:31-46 NIV

When the Son of Man comes in His glory, and all the angels with Him, He will sit on His glorious throne. All the nations will be gathered before Him, and He will separate the people one from another as a shepherd separates the sheep from the goats. He will put the sheep on His right and the goats on His left.

Then the King will say to those on His right, "Come, you who are blessed by My Father; take your inheritance, the kingdom prepared for you since the creation of the world. For I was hungry and you gave Me something to eat, I was thirsty and you gave Me something to drink, I was a stranger and you invited Me in, I needed clothes and you clothed Me, I was sick and you looked after Me, I was in prison and you came to visit Me."

Then the righteous will answer Him, "Lord, when did we see You hungry and feed You, or thirsty and give You something to drink? When did we see You a stranger and invite You in, or needing clothes and clothe You? When did we see You sick or in prison and go to visit You?"

The King will reply, "Truly I tell you, whatever you did for one of the least of these brothers and sisters of Mine, you did for Me."

Then He will say to those on His left, "Depart from Me, you who are cursed, into the eternal fire prepared for the devil and his angels. For I was hungry and you gave Me nothing to eat, I was thirsty and you gave Me nothing to drink, I was a stranger and you did not invite Me in, I needed clothes and you did not clothe Me, I was sick and in prison and you did not look after Me."

They also will answer, "Lord, when did we see You hungry or thirsty or a stranger or needing clothes or sick or in prison, and did not help You?"

He will reply, "Truly I tell you, whatever you did not do for one of the least of these, you did not do for Me."

Then they will go away to eternal punishment, but the righteous to eternal life.

Have we placed
a hierarchy on
who receives our
compassion and,
depending upon
that, we determine
when to act?

"I tell you the truth, when you refused to help the least of these My brothers and sisters, you were refusing to help Me." Reading this and imagining Jesus saying it to me nearly breaks my heart. It makes me get defensive, and I want to rise up as I exclaim, "No, Jesus! Of course I would do those things for You! I would do anything for You!" However, once my pride goes down and my awareness of my own flesh rises, I realize that there are many times that I miss the opportunity to serve others and represent Jesus to them. Why is it that I place less value on someone I don't seemingly recognize, but if it were Jesus right there, I would be quick to the draw? Have I placed a hierarchy on who receives my compassion and, depending upon that, determine when to act?

I don't mean for this commentary to be discouraging, as we all can raise our hands when asked if we have bypassed Jesus through bypassing other people. Rather, reading these Scriptures, the eyes of my heart are enlightened to the possibilities and opportunities to be His hands and feet. The tendency for us to determine if someone around us is worthy of our generosity or compassion is removed; the answer is simply yes.

I don't know about you, but I don't want to live my life so consumed by my own desires—none of which fulfill the longing to serve and look like Jesus—that I realize only when I get to the end that the richest part was the people along the way.

> *Reading these Scriptures,
> the eyes of my heart are
> enlightened to the possibilities
> and opportunities to be
> His hands and feet.*

PONDER HIS LOVE

1. *Have you ever considered the consequences of what we do or don't do for those in need to be so great?*

2. *Why do you think Jesus says, "Whatever you did for one of the least of these brothers and sisters of Mine, you did for Me"? Do His words help you understand how to meet with Jesus where He is looking for you?*

3. *Jesus defines "the righteous" and "the blessed" through their actions. What recent actions of yours do you think would please the Lord? What actions are you stirred to take in the days ahead?*

4. *Thinking about your current pace and rhythm, do they allow you the time and space to see those who might be in need around you?*

5. *When reading this story, who is the first person or what is the first cause that comes to your mind? We often have a burdened heart for particular people groups and places. Pay attention to that.*

Hey Jesus, thank You for this call-out for compassion. My heart, soul, and mind needed to be reminded of this truth. How easily I can put my needs above others or make assumptions of how others got to the place that they are. I'm so sorry for forgetting that all Your people are to be esteemed, taken care of, and seen, regardless of their circumstances.

Will You make me quick to offer compassion? I want to go above and beyond, offering my time, resources, and energy to others. Help me see others as You see them and with the same filter that You see me—through the lens of righteousness—undeserved but free.

Inspire in me new ways to extend my gifts and what I have, not giving in to the temptation to believe that I don't have enough. You long to do much with my little. Help me be a person of praise and generosity, sparking the desire of others to give and serve too.

Most of all, Father, I ask for deep humility. The moment that I believe I am above another or that any type of service is below me, reel me in. Posture my heart at Your feet and help me see through Your eyes so that I can live in a way that honors You.

In the compassionate, generous, and humble name of Jesus, amen.

MEDITATE ON HIS LOVE

MICAH 6:8 NLT

No, O people, the LORD has told you what is good, and this is what He requires of you: to do what is right, to love mercy, and to walk humbly with your God.

ROMANS 12:8 NIV

If it is to encourage, then give encouragement; if it is giving, then give generously; if it is to lead, do it diligently; if it is to show mercy, do it cheerfully.

LUKE 22:27 NIV

For who is greater, the one who is at the table or the one who serves? Is it not the one who is at the table? But I am among you as one who serves.

JAMES 5:11 NIV

As you know, we count as blessed those who have persevered. You have heard of Job's perseverance and have seen what the Lord finally brought about. The Lord is full of compassion and mercy.

COLOSSIANS 3:23-24 NIV

Whatever you do, work at it with all your heart, as working for the Lord, not for human masters, since you know that you will receive an inheritance from the Lord as a reward. It is the Lord Christ you are serving.

LEARN ABOUT HIS LOVE

Planted in Good Ground

MARK 4:1–34 NLT

**PARABLE OF THE FARMER
SCATTERING SEED**

Once again Jesus began teaching by the lakeshore. A very large crowd soon gathered around Him, so He got into a boat. Then He sat in the boat while all the people remained on the shore. He taught them by telling many stories in the form of parables, such as this one:

"Listen! A farmer went out to plant some seed. As he scattered it across his field, some of the seed fell on a footpath, and the birds came and ate it. Other seed fell on shallow soil with underlying rock. The seed sprouted quickly because the soil was shallow. But the plant soon wilted under the hot sun, and since it didn't have deep roots, it died. Other seed fell among thorns that grew up and choked out the tender plants so they produced no grain. Still other seeds fell on fertile soil, and they sprouted, grew, and produced a crop that was thirty, sixty, and even a hundred times as much as had been planted!" Then He said, "Anyone with ears to hear should listen and understand."

Later, when Jesus was alone with the twelve disciples and with the others who were gathered around, they asked Him what the parables meant.

He replied, "You are permitted to understand the secret of the Kingdom of God. But I use parables for everything I say to outsiders, so that the Scriptures might be fulfilled: 'When they see what I do, they will learn nothing. When they hear what I say, they will not understand. Otherwise, they will turn to Me and be forgiven.'"

Then Jesus said to them, "If you can't understand the meaning of this parable, how will you understand all the other parables? The farmer plants seed by taking God's word to others. The seed that fell on the footpath represents those who hear the message, only to have Satan come at once and take it away. The seed on the rocky soil represents those who hear the message and immediately receive it with joy. But since they don't have deep roots, they don't last long. They fall away as soon as they have problems or are persecuted for believing God's word. The seed that fell among the thorns represents others who hear God's word, but all too quickly the message is crowded out by the worries of this life, the lure of wealth, and the desire for other things, so no fruit is produced. And the seed that fell on good soil represents those who hear and accept God's word and produce a harvest of thirty, sixty, or even a hundred times as much as had been planted!"

PARABLE OF THE LAMP

Then Jesus asked them, "Would anyone light a lamp and then put it under a basket or under a bed? Of course not! A lamp is placed on a stand, where its light will shine. For everything that is hidden will eventually be brought into the open, and every secret will be brought to light. Anyone with ears to hear should listen and understand."

Then he added, "Pay close attention to what you hear. The closer you listen, the more understanding you will be given—and you will receive even more. To those who listen to My teaching, more understanding will be given. But for those who are not listening, even what little understanding they have will be taken away from them.

PARABLE OF THE GROWING SEED

Jesus also said, "The Kingdom of God is like a farmer who scatters seed on the ground. Night and day, while he's asleep or awake, the seed sprouts and grows, but he does not understand how it happens. The earth produces the crops on its own. First a leaf blade pushes through, then the heads of wheat are formed, and finally the grain ripens. And as soon as the grain is ready, the farmer comes and harvests it with a sickle, for the harvest time has come."

PARABLE OF THE MUSTARD SEED

Jesus said, "How can I describe the Kingdom of God? What story should I use to illustrate it? It is like a mustard seed planted in the ground. It is the smallest of all seeds, but it becomes the largest of all garden plants; it grows long branches, and birds can make nests in its shade."

Jesus used many similar stories and illustrations to teach the people as much as they could understand. In fact, in His public ministry He never taught without using parables; but afterward, when He was alone with His disciples, He explained everything to them.

I love how Jesus uses parables that include such visual representations to teach His disciples. This one allows us to imagine three different scenarios: a seed planted on shallow soil, a seed planted in thorns and rocks, and a seed planted on fertile soil. Jesus uses this parable to explain the necessity of not just hearing the Word of God but establishing ourselves in the truth of what it says.

His explanation demonstrates that it is not the size or type of seed that determines its success; rather, it is the soil in which it grows. Sometimes I struggle with comparing what I have to those around me or wondering if the predicted forecast will keep me from experiencing the blooming flowers that I hope my life will produce. However, this parable says that when we plant ourselves in the fertile soil of God's Word and character, our lives will display His glory.

Is there anyone who desires our fruitfulness, contentment, and growth more than the One who made us? Not even close. As we abide in Him, we experience His heart for us—formed through grace, carried with strength, and laced with gentleness. When we really come to understand this truth, we will want to tell everyone about the ultimate Farmer! The One who takes all our efforts and turns them into something that will shake the world.

When we plant
ourselves in the fertile
soil of God's Word and
character, our lives
will display His glory.

1. *Do you see similarities in thorny or rocky soil, a lamp under a basket, and those who are not listening? How do these examples help us understand our own responses to Jesus?*

2. *Are there seasons in your life when the Word fell on good soil and others when it fell "among thorns"? How did you move past the thorny soil to more fertile soil?*

3. What is the biggest obstacle that keeps you from digging into the Word and growing deeper roots?

4. When you read the phrase "For everything that is hidden will eventually be brought into the open," what is the first thing that comes to your mind? Why?

5. What is one specific way that you can fertilize your soil so that your life can be good ground?

Dear Lord, thank You for these parables that teach me about what You desire for my life and how to pursue righteousness. I really want to be someone who hears Your Word and takes it seriously, knowing that life is not found outside its boundaries. Will You help me cultivate good ground so that I can be deeply rooted, finding my identity in You and You alone?

Sometimes I find myself so desperately wanting results that are visible and quantifiable to a watching world that I am tempted to plant my seeds in shallow ground. However, I know that You would much rather I spend the time digging up the rocks underneath the surface so that my roots extend deep into Your love. Uncover what must be uncovered and expose what You must so that I can live a life that points to You. Thank You for helping me find forgiveness and freedom when my desires lead me to shallow places. Thank You for never making me feel guilty when You have to refine me.

In the moments when the thorns seem like they're bleeding the life out of me, help me pursue health and restoration, no matter the cost. Thank You for feeling the weight of my worries with me, while never allowing me to be a victim of my life.

I commit my way to You, Father. Your Word is everything pure, true, and kind. Help me yearn for wisdom, knowing that it is far greater than silver or gold. Planted deep in Your grace and watered by Your Word, my life is good ground for Your kingdom. In Jesus' name, amen.

MEDITATE ON HIS LOVE

JEREMIAH 17:8 ESV

He is like a tree planted by water, that sends out its roots by the stream, and does not fear when heat comes, for its leaves remain green, and is not anxious in the year of drought, for it does not cease to bear fruit.

PSALM 1:3 ESV

He is like a tree planted by streams of water that yields its fruit in its season, and its leaf does not wither. In all that he does, he prospers.

ISAIAH 40:8 NIV

The grass withers and the flowers fall, but the word of our God endures forever.

MATTHEW 7:24 NIV

Therefore everyone who hears these words of Mine and puts them into practice is like a wise man who built his house on the rock.

LUKE 11:28 NIV

He replied, "Blessed rather are those who hear the word of God and obey it."

LEARN ABOUT HIS LOVE

Dedicated to Serve

JOHN 13:1-38 NLT

Before the Passover celebration, Jesus knew that His hour had come to leave this world and return to His Father. He had loved His disciples during His ministry on earth, and now He loved them to the very end. It was time for supper, and the devil had already prompted Judas, son of Simon Iscariot, to betray Jesus. Jesus knew that the Father had given Him authority over everything and that He had come from God and would return to God. So he got up from the table, took off His robe, wrapped a towel around His waist, and poured water into a basin. Then He began to wash the disciples' feet, drying them with the towel He had around Him.

When Jesus came to Simon Peter, Peter said to Him, "Lord, are You going to wash my feet?"

Jesus replied, "You don't understand now what I am doing, but someday you will."

"No," Peter protested, "You will never ever wash my feet!"

Jesus replied, "Unless I wash you, you won't belong to Me."

Simon Peter exclaimed, "Then wash my hands and head as well, Lord, not just my feet!"

Jesus replied, "A person who has bathed all over does not need to wash, except for the feet, to be entirely clean. And you disciples are clean, but not all of you." For Jesus knew who would betray Him. That is what He meant when He said, "Not all of you are clean."

After washing their feet, He put on His robe again and sat down and asked, "Do you understand what I was doing? You call me 'Teacher' and 'Lord,' and you are right, because that's what I am. And since I, your Lord and Teacher, have washed your feet, you ought to wash each other's feet. I have given you an example to follow. Do as I have done to you. I tell you the truth, slaves are not greater than their master. Nor is the messenger more important than the one who sends the message. Now that you know these things, God will bless you for doing them.

JESUS PREDICTS HIS BETRAYAL

"I am not saying these things to all of you; I know the ones I have chosen. But this fulfills the Scripture that says, 'The one who eats My food has turned against Me.' I tell you this beforehand, so that when it happens you will believe that I am the Messiah. I tell you the truth, anyone who welcomes My messenger is welcoming Me, and anyone who welcomes Me is welcoming the Father who sent Me."

Now Jesus was deeply troubled, and He exclaimed, "I tell you the truth, one of you will betray Me!"

The disciples looked at each other, wondering whom He could mean. The disciple Jesus loved was sitting next to Jesus at the table. Simon Peter motioned to him to ask, "Who's He talking about?" So that disciple leaned over to Jesus and asked, "Lord, who is it?"

Jesus responded, "It is the one to whom I give the bread I dip in the bowl." And when He had dipped it, He gave it to Judas, son of Simon Iscariot. When Judas had eaten the bread, Satan entered into him. Then Jesus told him, "Hurry and do what you're going to do." None of the others at the table knew what Jesus meant. Since Judas was their treasurer, some thought Jesus was telling him to go and pay for the food or to give some money to the poor. So Judas left at once, going out into the night.

JESUS PREDICTS PETER'S DENIAL

As soon as Judas left the room, Jesus said, "The time has come for the Son of Man to enter into His glory, and God will be glorified because of Him. And since God receives glory because of the Son, He will give His own glory to the Son, and He will do so at once. Dear children, I will be with you only a little longer. And as I told the Jewish leaders, you will search for Me, but you can't come where I am going. So now I am giving you a new commandment: Love each other. Just as I have loved you, you should love each other. Your love for one another will prove to the world that you are My disciples."

Simon Peter asked, "Lord, where are You going?"

And Jesus replied, "You can't go with Me now, but you will follow Me later."

"But why can't I come now, Lord?" he asked. "I'm ready to die for You."

Jesus answered, "Die for Me? I tell you the truth, Peter—before the rooster crows tomorrow morning, you will deny three times that you even know Me."

The notion that the leader and teacher would be the One washing the feet of His followers was outlandish during this time. This task was seen as the lowest of the low but a very necessary practice in order to be clean. Thinking about this, I wonder what the disciples were thinking as Jesus bent down in front of the first disciple and began washing his feet. Were they confused? Shocked? Or relatively unsurprised because they had seen Jesus disregard so many societal norms up to this point?

Taking this visual representation and applying it to my own life, I find it challenging to implement and see what it would require from me. Not to mention, if I knew that the very people I was going to serve would deny me just days later, it seems impossible. I love that Jesus didn't assume any personal offense in this story; He knew that His serving the disciples pointed to the love of His heavenly Father, and He was not going to do anything to compromise that.

That's my hope for myself—and for you—that we would care so much about others discovering that they are loved by Jesus, we would stop worrying about proving a point, social status, or anything that would keep us from grabbing the towel, humbling our hearts, and serving them.

He knew that His serving the disciples pointed to the love of His heavenly Father, and He was not going to do anything to compromise that.

PONDER HIS LOVE

1. *Jesus washed the disciples' feet as one of His last acts before He was crucified because He wanted to demonstrate the importance of serving others. What are some current ways that you serve others?*

2. *It says that "Jesus was deeply troubled" before He talked about one of the disciples betraying Him, but He didn't let His emotions keep Him from serving them. What do you do when your emotions get in the way of showing up for others?*

3. *Has there been a time when you knew something was about to happen (like the disciples knowing Jesus was leaving) that would change your life? How did it feel?*

4. *If someone surveyed your recent actions, words, and lifestyle, would they say that you represent the statement, "Your love for one another will prove to the world that You are My disciples"?*

5. *Do you think Jesus washed everyone's feet in the room together so that they would all have accountability to serve one another in love? Who in your life is willing to call you to this truth?*

Dear Lord, thank You for this story and the way that it encourages and directs my spirit. When I imagine myself in the room with the disciples and You as You washed everyone's feet, I am overwhelmed with gratitude. I see You taking off Your robe, sitting lowly on the floor, and taking Your hard-working hands to wash my feet, and nothing makes sense. How is it that the King of the world not only gifted me with breath but then made it His mission to equip me to serve Him on this side of heaven? Your mercy is too great, Father.

Will You humble my spirit so that I can serve others like You did? Show me how to wash others' feet in a very practical sense. What does this world need that I have? Where do I place my time and my energy? How can I get uncomfortable so that You can be made great within me? Build in me an unwavering commitment to Your people, regardless of what is reciprocated to me. Show me how to love all-inclusively and well, not showing favoritism or forgetfulness.

Lord, I know I will deny, betray, and reject You in moments. I hate that my flesh is so quick to run from the One it was created to pursue. When I mess up, will You help me repent quickly? Quicken my steps back to You and heal my heart so that I can love others like You. I am Your disciple, available and loved by You.

In the humble and cleansing name of Jesus, amen.

MEDITATE ON HIS LOVE

GALATIANS 5:13 NIV

You, my brothers and sisters, were called to be free. But do not use your freedom to indulge the flesh; rather, serve one another humbly in love.

JOHN 12:26 NIV

Whoever serves me must follow me; and where I am, my servant also will be. My Father will honor the one who serves me.

HEBREWS 9:14 NIV

How much more, then, will the blood of Christ, who through the eternal Spirit offered Himself unblemished to God, cleanse our consciences from acts that lead to death, so that we may serve the living God!

MARK 10:45 NIV

For even the Son of Man did not come to be served, but to serve, and to give His life as a ransom for many.

LEARN ABOUT HIS LOVE

Renewed by Mercy

JOHN 8:1-30 NIV

But Jesus went to the Mount of Olives. At dawn He appeared again in the temple courts, where all the people gathered around Him, and He sat down to teach them. The teachers of the law and the Pharisees brought in a woman caught in adultery. They made her stand before the group and said to Jesus, "Teacher, this woman was caught in the act of adultery. In the Law Moses commanded us to stone such women. Now what do You say?" They were using this question as a trap, in order to have a basis for accusing Him.

But Jesus bent down and started to write on the ground with His finger. When they kept on questioning Him, He straightened up and said to them, "Let any one of you who is without sin be the first to throw a stone at her." Again He stooped down and wrote on the ground.

At this, those who heard began to go away one at a time, the older ones first, until only Jesus was left, with the woman still standing there. Jesus straightened up and asked her, "Woman, where are they? Has no one condemned you?"

"No one, sir," she said.

"Then neither do I condemn you," Jesus declared. "Go now and leave your life of sin."

When Jesus spoke again to the people, He said, "I am the light of the world. Whoever follows me will never walk in darkness, but will have the light of life."

The Pharisees challenged Him, "Here You are, appearing as Your own witness; Your testimony is not valid."

Jesus answered, "Even if I testify on My own behalf, My testimony is valid, for I know where I came from and where I am going. But you have no idea where I come from or where I am going. You judge by human standards; I pass judgment on no one. But if I do judge, My decisions are true, because I am not alone. I stand with the Father, who sent Me. In your own Law it is written that the testimony of two witnesses is true. I am one who testifies for myself; My other witness is the Father, who sent Me."

Then they asked Him, "Where is Your father?"

"You do not know Me or My Father," Jesus replied. "If you knew Me, you would know My Father also." He spoke these words while teaching in the temple courts near the place where the offerings were put. Yet no one seized Him, because His hour had not yet come.

DISPUTE OVER WHO JESUS IS

Once more Jesus said to them, "I am going away, and you will look for Me, and you will die in your sin. Where I go, you cannot come."

This made the Jews ask, "Will He kill himself? Is that why He says, 'Where I go, you cannot come'?"

But He continued, "You are from below; I am from above. You are of this world; I am not of this world. I told you that you would die in your sins; if you do not believe that I am He, you will indeed die in your sins."

"Who are You?" they asked.

"Just what I have been telling you from the beginning," Jesus replied. "I have much to say in judgment of you. But He who sent Me is trustworthy, and what I have heard from Him I tell the world."

They did not understand that He was telling them about His Father. So Jesus said, "When you have lifted up the Son of Man, then you will know that I am He and that I do nothing on My own but speak just what the Father has taught Me. The One who sent Me is with Me; He has not left Me alone, for I always do what pleases Him." Even as He spoke, many believed in Him.

Imagining this story in modern times, I can see myself in both the Pharisees and the adulterous woman. That may seem strong to say, but I think if we are honest, we can all place ourselves in both roles. The Pharisees are critical and judgmental; their job is protecting religious law. They believed the way to please God was by following a long list of rules and regulations, but by focusing on the law, they completely missed the true meaning of God's love and power. The adulterous woman has been living a life of sin and knows her actions led her to a fate she never intended.

In my own life, there have been times when I tried to flip the mirror and focus on the sins of those in front of me. It felt easier. Self-preservation, or so I thought. However, not once did this prove to help me or them; it confined both of us to the rigidity of religion instead of the richness of relationship. And in other moments, I have been the adulterous woman, doing the very things I know Jesus wouldn't approve of and fearing the consequences. Reflecting on some of these times, I can feel the self-condemnation and pain. Why is it that we beat ourselves up, only to go do the same things again?

But then we see Jesus. Isn't it just like Him to flip the script and make everyone stop in their tracks? His response to the Pharisees forces them to look in the mirror and realize the mercy they themselves have received. Seeing how Jesus responds to this woman confirms that as His people, we must never let religion keep us from seeing someone, speaking life into them, and extending mercy far greater than they deserve.

We must never let religion keep us from seeing someone, speaking life into them, and extending mercy far greater than they deserve.

1. *Why do you think Jesus bent down and started drawing in the sand instead of looking the Pharisees directly in the eye?*

2. *Why do you think Jesus didn't directly confront the woman's adulterous behavior? Do you think He simply said "life of sin" because He knew that she knew what He was referring to?*

3. *Have you experienced times where your religion has gotten in the way of your ability to extend mercy in a relationship? How did you handle that?*

4. *After Jesus said, "Let any one of you who is without sin be the first to throw a stone at her," who were the first people to leave? Why do you think that is?*

5. *Has there been a time in your life when you have felt such judgment and condemnation? How did Jesus' mercy help you move forward or experience healing?*

Dear Lord, reading about the way You bend down to see Your people and cover them with mercy blankets my spirit with peace. I am so grateful for this reminder, as at times I can see myself in both the Pharisee and the adulterous woman in this story. Will You bring to light anything that might be keeping me in shame or condemnation? Sometimes I don't even realize that I am hiding certain parts of my life or who I am; show me what is hidden.

As the light floods in, remind me that I am safe under the shadow of Your wings. I don't have to fear what others say because I know what You say about me. And Jesus, if it is me who is condemning another, convict my soul. Have I not received unending mercy and grace myself? Lead me back to the cross where Your forgiveness gave me life.

Thank You for always taking the time to see me and come to my defense. If You are for me, who can be against me? When You speak, empower me to act on what You say. Freedom, healing, and mercy are what You offer.

Counsel me in giving this same kind of mercy to those around me. Remaining unthreatened by accusations, fear, or judgment, may I learn how to offer Your compassion to a hurting world.

In the mighty and merciful name of Jesus, amen.

MEDITATE ON HIS LOVE

HEBREWS 4:16 ESV

Let us then with confidence draw near to the throne of grace, that we may receive mercy and find grace to help in time of need.

LUKE 6:36–37 ESV

Be merciful, even as your Father is merciful. Judge not, and you will not be judged; condemn not, and you will not be condemned; forgive, and you will be forgiven.

TITUS 3:5 ESV

He saved us, not because of works done by us in righteousness, but according to his own mercy, by the washing of regeneration and renewal of the Holy Spirit.

MICAH 7:18 ESV

Who is a God like you, pardoning iniquity and passing over transgression for the remnant of his inheritance? He does not retain his anger forever, because he delights in steadfast love.

MATTHEW 5:7 ESV

Blessed are the merciful, for they shall receive mercy.

For more on this topic, scan the QR code for a video message from Cleere.

LEARN ABOUT HIS LOVE

Purified from the Inside Out

MATTHEW 15:1-20 NIV

Then some Pharisees and teachers of the law came to Jesus from Jerusalem and asked, "Why do your disciples break the tradition of the elders? They don't wash their hands before they eat!"

Jesus replied, "And why do you break the command of God for the sake of your tradition? For God said, 'Honor your father and mother' and 'Anyone who curses their father or mother is to be put to death.' But you say that if anyone declares that what might have been used to help their father or mother is 'devoted to God,' they are not to 'honor their father or mother' with it. Thus you nullify the word of God for the sake of your tradition. You hypocrites! Isaiah was right when he prophesied about you:

'These people honor me with their lips, but
*   their hearts are far from me.*

They worship me in vain;
*   their teachings are merely human rules.'*

Jesus called the crowd to Him and said, "Listen and understand. What goes into someone's mouth does not defile them, but what comes out of their mouth, that is what defiles them." Then the disciples came to Him and asked, "Do you know that the Pharisees were offended when they heard this?" He replied, "Every plant that my heavenly Father has not planted will be pulled up by the roots. Leave them; they are blind guides. If the blind lead the blind, both will fall into a pit." Peter said, "Explain the parable to us." "Are you still so dull?" Jesus asked them. "Don't you see that whatever enters the mouth goes into the stomach and then out of the body? But the things that come out of a person's mouth come from the heart, and these defile them. For out of the heart come evil thoughts— murder, adultery, sexual immorality, theft, false testimony, slander. These are what defile a person; but eating with unwashed hands does not defile them."

Do you think
our religion and
obsession with rules
can get in the way
of experiencing the
heart of Jesus?

Jesus is quick to the draw, isn't He? Reading this story, I am kind of blown away by His response to the disciples and the Pharisees. He doesn't mince words or give anyone a break; however, His mercy is still evident because He greatly desires for the disciples to understand that the Pharisees' hearts are hardened. They have become so used to catering the law to fit their lives that they fail to base their lives on the heart of the law.

What stands out to me in this story is the way that it begins. The Pharisees witness the disciples eating with uncleansed hands, and that is how they approach Jesus—attacking Him by attacking His people. Their focus is on criticizing how other people operate rather than really understanding the heart of the God who wrote the laws they say are being broken. I think Jesus' biggest frustration is that the Pharisees are tossing around the laws of God as if they are ammo rather than realizing they themselves desperately need His saving grace.

Jesus speaks to the inside versus the outside and what truly counts. He is most worried about what we look like on the inside: Are we pure? Do we love Him? Do we desire to resemble Him and love His people? In a culture that focuses so much time on the way we present our lives, I pray we don't strive to earn favor at the expense of being with Jesus and resting in that love. Laws help guide, but only love can purify the heart.

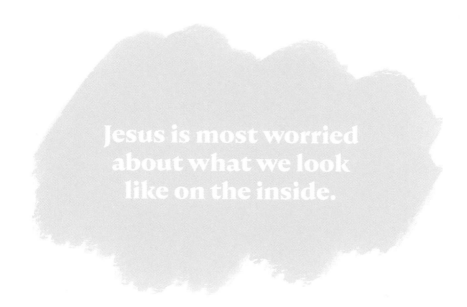

Jesus is most worried about what we look like on the inside.

1. *The Pharisees are so distracted by the laws that they miss the very reason and authority behind them. Do you think our religion and obsession with rules can get in the way of experiencing the heart of Jesus?*

2. *Jesus said the Pharisees were manipulating the Scriptures to fit their lives. Have you taken a Scripture out of context before? How did it affect what you did? Were there any consequences?*

3. In our current culture, we struggle to understand God's purpose behind child hunger, pandemics, and unstable political climates. We are all trying to figure out what to do. How do you think you should go about seeking understanding? Do you think you sometimes miss the mark?

4. Jesus says that it is what comes out of a man that defiles him, not what goes in. He is referring to how a person's heart health is more important than any law we try not to break. How is your heart health? What has been coming out of you?

5. Jesus responds to His disciples saying, "Are you still so dull?" What tone do you think Jesus said this in? Why?

Dear Lord, thank You for this story and Your constant reminders of where to focus. Sometimes I am quick to point out the ways others are failing and sometimes I am still confused about what You desire for my life, even though You have been so clear.

Will You show me how to pursue having a pure heart? I know Your law is guidance and wisdom, but Your transforming grace is what makes my life possible. Help me to keep my eyes on my own journey and how I can spread Your kindness to others. It is not my job to be another person's Holy Spirit. You can handle that responsibility.

When life feels unfair, situations are not optimal, or I am struggling, remind me that while I may not be able to control circumstances or prevent my heart from experiencing something, I do decide how I respond to it. You have given me the authority and power to choose what comes out—words of grace, actions of humility, songs of deliverance, and ways of trust. Guard my heart and give me discernment so that I can know when to close a door and when to leave it open.

Thank You for cleansing every part of me, leaving no part of me unclean. You are not afraid of any dirt I bring to Your throne; You wash, restore, and breathe life into me. White as snow, that is what You make me.

I want to be consumed by Your love, knowing that as long as I abide in You, I will produce fruit and hope.

In the purifying, accepting, and hope-giving name of Jesus, amen.

MEDITATE ON HIS LOVE

EPHESIANS 4:25–29 NIV

Therefore each of you must put off falsehood and speak truthfully to his neighbor for we are all members of one body. In your anger do not sin. Do not let the sun go down while you are still angry, and do not give the devil a foothold. He who has been stealing must steal no longer, but must work, doing something useful with his own hands, that he may have something to share with those in need. Do not let any unwholesome talk come out of your mouths, but only what is helpful for building others up according to their needs, that it may benefit those who listen.

MATTHEW 12:34–37 NIV

For the mouth speaks what the heart is full of. A good man brings good things out of the good stored up in him, and an evil man brings evil things out of the evil stored up in him. But I tell you that everyone will have to give account on the day of judgment for every empty word they have spoken. For by your words you will be acquitted, and by your words you will be condemned.

JAMES 2:14–17 NIV

What good is it, my brothers and sisters, if someone claims to have faith but has no deeds? Can such faith save them? Suppose a brother or a sister is without clothes and daily food. If one of you says to them, "Go in peace; keep warm and well fed," but does nothing about their physical needs, what good is it? In the same way, faith by itself, if it is not accompanied by action, is dead.

JAMES 4:11–12 NIV

Brothers and sisters, do not slander one another. Anyone who speaks against a brother or sister or judges them speaks against the law and judges it. When you judge the law, you are not keeping it, but sitting in judgment on it. There is only one Lawgiver and Judge, the One who is able to save and destroy. But you—who are you to judge your neighbor?

I PETER 2:1–3 NIV

Therefore, rid yourselves of all malice and all deceit, hypocrisy, envy, and slander of every kind. Like newborn babies, crave pure spiritual milk, so that by it you may grow up in your salvation, now that you have tasted that the Lord is good.

LEARN ABOUT HIS LOVE

Pursued by Reckless Love

JOSHUA 2:1–24 NIV

Then Joshua son of Nun secretly sent two spies from Shittim. "Go, look over the land," he said, "especially Jericho." So they went and entered the house of a prostitute named Rahab and stayed there.

The king of Jericho was told, "Look, some of the Israelites have come here tonight to spy out the land." So the king of Jericho sent this message to Rahab: "Bring out the men who came to you and entered your house, because they have come to spy out the whole land."

But the woman had taken the two men and hidden them. She said, "Yes, the men came to me, but I did not know where they had come from. At dusk, when it was time to close the city gate, they left. I don't know which way they went. Go after them quickly. You may catch up with them." (But she had taken them up to the roof and hidden them under the stalks of flax she had laid out on the roof.) So the men set out in pursuit of the spies on the road that leads to the fords of the Jordan, and as soon as the pursuers had gone out, the gate was shut.

Before the spies lay down for the night, she went up on the roof and said to them, "I know that the LORD has given you this land and that a great fear of you has fallen on us, so that all who live in this country are melting in fear because of you. We have heard how the LORD dried up the water of the Red Sea for you when you came out of Egypt, and what you did to Sihon and Og, the two kings of the Amorites east of the Jordan, whom you completely destroyed. When we heard of it, our hearts melted in fear and everyone's courage failed because of you, for the LORD your God is God in heaven above and on the earth below.

"Now then, please swear to me by the LORD that you will show kindness to my family, because I have shown kindness to you. Give me a sure sign that you will spare the lives of my father and mother, my brothers and sisters, and all who belong to them—and that you will save us from death."

"Our lives for your lives!" the men assured her. "If you don't tell what we are doing, we will treat you kindly and faithfully when the LORD gives us the land."

So she let them down by a rope through the window, for the house she lived in was part of the city wall. She said to them, "Go to the hills so the pursuers will not find you. Hide yourselves there three days until they return, and then go on your way."

Now the men had said to her, "This oath you made us swear will not be binding on us unless, when we enter the land, you have tied this scarlet cord in the window through which you let us down, and unless you have brought your father and mother, your brothers and all your family into your house. If any of them go outside your house into the street, their blood will be on their own heads; we will not be responsible. As for those who are in the house with you, their blood will be on our head if a hand is laid on them. But if you tell what we are doing, we will be released from the oath you made us swear."

"Agreed," she replied. "Let it be as you say."

So she sent them away, and they departed. And she tied the scarlet cord in the window.

When they left, they went into the hills and stayed there three days, until the pursuers had searched all along the road and returned without finding them. Then the two men started back. They went down out of the hills, forded the river and came to Joshua son of Nun and told him everything that had happened to them. They said to Joshua, "The LORD has surely given the whole land into our hands; all the people are melting in fear because of us."

Rahab was a harlot. To downplay the life of sin she had been living would be to also downplay the grace of God that is woven into this story. It's just like our Jesus to use the very thing that was Rahab's stronghold to become the source of her freedom. It was because she had been entertaining travelers in her home along the wall of Jericho that she knew of the schemes that were underway in the land.

Though Rahab had been pursuing another lifestyle, God had still been pursuing her. When the spies came, Rahab had the discernment and faith to immediately know they were different. She put not only her own life on the line but the life of her family by willingly hiding the spies from their captors. This shows me that Rahab not only desired a better life for herself but that she already had the faith to risk her life for God. When Rahab protected the spies, who were believers, she was siding with God Himself.

Rahab later marries one of the spies she protects and lives an honorable life that is vastly different from the harlot label stamped upon her name in the beginning. This makes me ask myself the question, "Do I believe that God is real enough to sacrifice my life for Him?" Spies may never knock at my door, but my life will present many opportunities to sacrifice for my faith. What will I say?

> It's just like our Jesus to use the very thing that was Rahab's stronghold to become the source of her freedom.

1. *We know it was not by happenstance that the spies chose Rahab's house. Do you think God was already writing this story of redemption? What makes you think He was or wasn't?*

2. *Do you find it difficult to trust that God has made you a new creation? Has shame kept you from acting in faith? Why?*

3. Rahab asks the spies to spare her and her family in return for her sacrifice. What does this reveal about Rahab? About God?

4. What was the purpose of the scarlet cord? What does it remind you of?

5. Do you trust God to show up for you if you show up for Him? In other words, are you afraid to step out in faith in case He doesn't show up?

Dear Lord, thank You for this marvelous and beautiful story of Rahab—what courage, what grace, what faith!

It is incomprehensible to me that You know the faults of all of Your people, and yet You still love them. Not just love them but pursue them. Not just pursue them but equip them. Not just equip them but use them!

I am reminded that my past does not define me but my present will direct me. As You did with Rahab, will You give me supernatural discernment to know who and what to open my door and my heart to? And who and what not to open them to? If I trust that You are who You say You are, my filth is not too much for You.

Thank You for the gift and transformative power of faith. Will You inform and prepare my heart for how to act on the faith I claim to have, not just speak about it? I want my life to be so desperate for Your rescue that I sacrifice everything You ask of me.

Just like Rahab's home, You are able to take a place that was full of sin and shame and restore it to a place of faith and fortitude. You rewrite the banner over my life, place me on sure ground, and help me become a person that looks like You.

Alert my spirit, Lord. Show me the "spies"—the opportunities to partner with You because I am so hidden in Your heart.

In the strong and faith-inspiring name of Jesus, amen.

MEDITATE ON HIS LOVE

HEBREWS 11:31 KJV

By faith the harlot Rahab perished not with them that believed not, when she received the spies with peace.

JOHN 17:17 ESV

Sanctify them in the truth; your word is truth.

PSALM 18:2 ESV

The LORD is my rock and my fortress and my deliverer, my God, my rock, in whom I take refuge, my shield, and the horn of my salvation, my stronghold.

ROMANS 5:1 ESV

Therefore, since we have been justified by faith, we have peace with God through our Lord Jesus Christ.

1 JOHN 3:16 ESV

By this we know love, that he laid down his life for us, and we ought to lay down our lives for the brothers.

LEARN ABOUT HIS LOVE

Strengthened as Usual

DANIEL 6:1-23 NLT

DANIEL IN THE LIONS' DEN

Darius the Mede decided to divide the kingdom into 120 provinces, and he appointed a high officer to rule over each province. The king also chose Daniel and two others as administrators to supervise the high officers and protect the king's interests. Daniel soon proved himself more capable than all the other administrators and high officers. Because of Daniel's great ability, the king made plans to place him over the entire empire.

Then the other administrators and high officers began searching for some fault in the way Daniel was handling government affairs, but they couldn't find anything to criticize or condemn. He was faithful, always responsible, and completely trustworthy. So they concluded, "Our only chance of finding grounds for accusing Daniel will be in connection with the rules of his religion."

So the administrators and high officers went to the king and said, "Long live King Darius! We are all in agreement—we administrators, officials, high officers, advisers, and governors—that the king should make a law that will be strictly enforced. Give orders that for

the next thirty days any person who prays to anyone, divine or human—except to you, Your Majesty—will be thrown into the den of lions. And now, Your Majesty, issue and sign this law so it cannot be changed, an official law of the Medes and Persians that cannot be revoked." So King Darius signed the law.

But when Daniel learned that the law had been signed, he went home and knelt down as usual in his upstairs room, with its windows open toward Jerusalem. He prayed three times a day, just as he had always done, giving thanks to his God. Then the officials went together to Daniel's house and found him praying and asking for God's help. So they went straight to the king and reminded him about his law. "Did you not sign a law that for the next thirty days any person who prays to anyone, divine or human—except to you, Your Majesty—will be thrown into the den of lions?"

"Yes," the king replied, "that decision stands; it is an official law of the Medes and Persians that cannot be revoked."

Then they told the king, "That man Daniel,

one of the captives from Judah, is ignoring you and your law. He still prays to his God three times a day."

Hearing this, the king was deeply troubled, and he tried to think of a way to save Daniel. He spent the rest of the day looking for a way to get Daniel out of this predicament.

In the evening the men went together to the king and said, "Your Majesty, you know that according to the law of the Medes and the Persians, no law that the king signs can be changed."

So at last the king gave orders for Daniel to be arrested and thrown into the den of lions. The king said to him, "May your God, whom you serve so faithfully, rescue you."

A stone was brought and placed over the mouth of the den. The king sealed the stone with his own royal seal and the seals of his nobles, so that no one could rescue Daniel. Then the king returned to his palace and spent the night fasting. He refused his usual entertainment and couldn't sleep at all that night.

Very early the next morning, the king got up and hurried out to the lions' den. When he got there, he called out in anguish, "Daniel, servant of the living God! Was your God, whom you serve so faithfully, able to rescue you from the lions?"

Daniel answered, "Long live the king! My God sent His angel to shut the lions' mouths so that they would not hurt me, for I have been found innocent in His sight. And I have not wronged you, Your Majesty."

The king was overjoyed and ordered that Daniel be lifted from the den. Not a scratch was found on him, for he had trusted in his God.

Honestly, when I first read this story, I thought to myself, *Why wouldn't God keep Daniel from having to enter the lions' den if Daniel is truly so obedient and faithful?* This seems like such an unfair and unjust situation. Daniel was known throughout the kingdom as a man of deep integrity, and his reward for it is being forsaken by the very One he served? However, my heart was reminded that opposition doesn't mean we are doing something wrong or going the wrong way; oftentimes, opposition solidifies that we are right in the middle of God's will.

After the law was made that required everyone to worship only the king, the Bible says, "He went home and knelt down *as usual*" (emphasis mine). My favorite two words in this entire Bible story might just be those two words: "as usual." Daniel did not panic because prayer was his continual posture.

This story immediately made me think about my own habits and ways I feed my faith. Do I assume my righteousness from yesterday poured over into today or do I seek Him continually? Do I let the circumstances I'm facing or the character of my God determine my faithfulness? I want to be like Daniel, showing up faithfully and declaring that my heavenly Father's opinion of me is the only one that matters. In doing so, I know that what the world may view as my setback will become a setup to once again prove that God is faithful and His Word is true.

I want to be like Daniel, showing up faithfully and declaring that my heavenly Father's opinion of me is the only one that matters.

1. *What is the equivalent of a lions' den in your life? Do you have a situation or circumstance that scares you or is threatening your joy? How do you plan to face it?*

2. *Scripture says, "Because of his great ability," Daniel was the one given reign over the entire kingdom. How have you seen how promotions, power, or advancement cause others to be jealous or spiteful?*

3. *Everyone referred to Daniel as the servant who obeyed God faithfully and yet he was still thrown into the den. Give an example of a time when you felt like you did what God asked yet got put in unfair circumstances. How did God show up during this time?*

4. *The king fasted, refused entertainment, and was restless the entire time Daniel was in the lions' den. Do you think God was working on his heart? What makes you think He was or wasn't?*

5. *How can you serve God more faithfully right where you are? What changes could you make?*

Dear Lord, thank You for this story about a man who didn't spend his life just talking about how good You are; rather, he spent his life walking in faithfulness and proving his trust in Your goodness. Will You help me meditate on Your Word and instruction as Daniel did? I want my life to align with the only standard that matters on this earth and in heaven.

As I prepare for each day, help me call out to You. Elevate my awareness of Your presence so that I may speak to it in everything that I do and say. When my emotions get the best of me and I'm frustrated with the view in front of me or the cards I have been dealt, remind me of the lions' den. I have no reason to fear opposition because You are with me, preserving my life and keeping me from harm.

Thank You for being faithful even when I'm faithless. How is it that You never waver from who You are? Your consistency, dependability, and grace are the foundation for my confidence. I want to declare Your goodness even when the world doesn't see it. Energize my soul with Your promises so that I can see my setbacks as setups for You to do what You do best.

Strengthen my resolve so that when others think of me, they think of someone who, like Daniel, does not stray from his Father's grip. What a blessing that would be.

In the powerful and faithful name of Jesus, amen.

MEDITATE ON HIS LOVE

HEBREWS 10:23 ESV

Let us hold fast the confession of our hope without wavering, for he who promised is faithful.

I SAMUEL 12:24 ESV

Only fear the LORD and serve him faithfully with all your heart. For consider what great things he has done for you

PSALM 89:8 ESV

O LORD God of hosts, who is mighty as you are, O Lord, with your faithfulness all around you?

DEUTERONOMY 7:9 ESV

Know therefore that the LORD your God is God, the faithful God who keeps covenant and steadfast love with those who love him and keep his commandments, to a thousand generations.

PROVERBS 20:6 ESV

Many a man proclaims his own steadfast love, but a faithful man who can find?

Accepted by Radical Love

MARK 9:33–50; LUKE 22:24–30 NIV

They came to Capernaum. When He was in the house, He asked them, "What were you arguing about on the road?" But they kept quiet because on the way they had argued about who was the greatest.

Sitting down, Jesus called the Twelve and said, "Anyone who wants to be first must be the very last, and the servant of all."

He took a little child whom He placed among them. Taking the child in His arms, He said to them, "Whoever welcomes one of these little children in My name welcomes Me; and whoever welcomes Me does not welcome Me but the One who sent Me."

WHOEVER IS NOT AGAINST US IS FOR US

"Teacher," said John, "we saw someone driving out demons in Your name and we told him to stop, because he was not one of us."

"Do not stop him," Jesus said. "For no one who does a miracle in My name can in the next moment say anything bad about Me, for whoever is not against us is for us. Truly I tell you, anyone who gives you a cup of water in My name because you belong to the Messiah will certainly not lose their reward.

CAUSING TO STUMBLE

"If anyone causes one of these little ones—those who believe in Me—to stumble, it would be better for them if a large millstone were hung around their neck and they were thrown into the sea. If your hand causes you to stumble, cut it off. It is better for you to enter life maimed than with two hands to go into hell, where the fire never goes out. And if your foot causes you to stumble, cut it off. It is better for you to enter life crippled than to have two feet and be thrown into hell. And if your eye causes you to stumble, pluck it out. It is better for you to enter the kingdom of God with one eye than to have two eyes and be thrown into hell, where the worms that eat them do not die, and the fire is not quenched. Everyone will be salted with fire. Salt is good, but if it loses its saltiness, how can you make it salty again? Have salt in yourselves, and be at peace with each other."

A dispute also arose among them as to which of them was considered to be greatest. Jesus said to them, "The kings of the Gentiles lord it over them; and those who exercise authority over them call themselves Benefactors. But you are not to be like that. Instead, the greatest among you should be like the youngest, and the one who rules like the one who serves. For who is greater, the one who is at the table or the one who serves? Is it not the one who is at the table? But I am among you as one who serves. You are those who have stood by Me in My trials. And I confer on you a kingdom, just as my Father conferred one on Me, so that you may eat and drink at My table in My kingdom and sit on thrones, judging the twelve tribes of Israel."

I love that Scripture tells us that the disciples were arguing about who was the greatest. It's as if Jesus knew we needed to be reminded that the disciples were human and sometimes mistakenly driven by their ego, too. In these passages, Jesus is talking with the disciples about who is great and what makes them great. Jesus pulls a child into the picture and says, "Whoever welcomes him, welcomes Me." What does He mean by this?

Later, the disciples tell Jesus that they told a man to stop casting out demons because he was not one of them. Jesus' response? Essentially, um, that is none of your business. Jesus reminds them that those that are not against Him are for Him. To me, I hear Jesus rolling out the banner of acceptance throughout these verses. What can a child offer the King of kings? Need. Dependence. Love based on both of these. Isn't this us? Isn't this what Jesus wants from us? He is unimpressed by the disciples' conversations about greatness and more impacted by the revelation of greatness that the child has.

It is because Jesus has accepted you and me that we even have the privilege, honor, and opportunity to accept others. What helps us be more accepting? Understanding the grace that we ourselves have been given and the tolerance the Father has for us. For if we are truly trying to spread the love of Christ, shouldn't we accept all people so that we can do our best to love them?

> It is because Jesus accepted you and me that we even have the privilege, honor, and opportunity to accept others.

PONDER HIS LOVE

1. *In Mark, when Jesus asks the disciples what they were arguing about, why do you think they grew silent? Is there someone in your life you're competing with to be the greatest? How is that going?*

2. *Scripture says that Jesus pulled into His arms a child who was already among them. Why do you think He did this? What did the disciples learn from this?*

3. *The disciples tried to stop the man who was casting out demons, but Jesus wasn't worried. Why do you think that is?*

4. *When Jesus talks about stumbling, He uses extreme language. Why do you think we dilute it to make ourselves more comfortable?*

5. *Regarding acceptance, do you fear being rejected? Do you ever wonder if God truly accepts you? Why or why not?*

Dear Lord, thank You for this story and the reminder of Your radical acceptance. I'm so grateful for the way You spoke to the disciples so that I can benefit from such wisdom.

Will You help me dive deeper into the acceptance You give my heart and soul? Understanding and grasping the lengths You go to cover me provides me with a greater ability to extend it to those around me. Help me demonstrate acceptance not just in my words and what I claim to believe but also in my everyday actions and responses.

You tell me to be like a child in order to enter Your gates. Father, I am Your child, dependent upon Your provision, desperate for Your attention, needy for Your touch, and hungry for Your approval. Thank You for raising me up to be strong in You but never letting me forget my role in our relationship.

Guide me as I celebrate the gifts of those around me, not looking to judge, condemn, or criticize what I am not a part of, as long as it is for Your kingdom. Like the man casting out demons, it is not my business to understand or solidify the gifts and edification of others. That is Your job.

Thank You for being a loving Father who draws my boundary lines and keeps me on solid ground. Help me be a person that pursues the light and adds salt to the world, providing truth and flavor.

In the accepting, kind, and forgiving name of Jesus, amen.

MEDITATE ON HIS LOVE

I JOHN 3:18 NIV

Dear children, let us not love with words or speech but with actions and in truth.

ROMANS 14:13 NIV

Therefore let us stop passing judgment on one another. Instead, make up your mind not to put any stumbling block or obstacle in the way of a brother or sister.

ROMANS 15:7 ESV

Therefore welcome one another as Christ has welcomed you, for the glory of God.

JUDE 24–25 NIV

To Him who is able to keep you from stumbling and to present you before His glorious presence without fault and with great joy—to the only God our Savior be glory, majesty, power and authority, through Jesus Christ our Lord, before all ages, now and forevermore! Amen.

GALATIANS 3:28 ESV

There is neither Jew nor Greek, there is neither slave nor free, there is no male and female, for you are all one in Christ Jesus.

LEARN ABOUT HIS LOVE

Devoted to His Desires

MARK 12:28-42; MATTHEW 22:34-45 NLT

THE MOST IMPORTANT COMMANDMENT

One of the teachers of religious law was standing there listening to the debate. He realized that Jesus had answered well, so he asked, "Of all the commandments, which is the most important?"

Jesus replied, "The most important commandment is this: 'Listen, O Israel! The Lord our God is the one and only Lord. And you must love the Lord your God with all your heart, all your soul, all your mind, and all your strength.' The second is equally important: 'Love your neighbor as yourself.' No other commandment is greater than these."

The teacher of religious law replied, "Well said, Teacher. You have spoken the truth by saying that there is only one God and no other. And I know it is important to love Him with all my heart and all my understanding and all my strength, and to love my neighbor as myself. This is more important than to offer all of the burnt offerings and sacrifices required in the law."

Realizing how much the man understood, Jesus said to him, "You are not far from the Kingdom of God." And after that, no one dared to ask Him any more questions.

WHOSE SON IS THE MESSIAH?

Later, as Jesus was teaching the people in the Temple, He asked, "Why do the teachers of religious law claim that the Messiah is the son of David? For David himself, speaking under the inspiration of the Holy Spirit, said, 'The LORD said to my Lord, Sit in the place of honor at My right hand until I humble your enemies beneath your feet.'

"Since David himself called the Messiah 'my Lord,' how can the Messiah be his son?" The large crowd listened to Him with great delight.

Jesus also taught: "Beware of these teachers of religious law! For they like to parade around in flowing robes and receive respectful greetings as they walk in the marketplaces. And how they love the seats of honor in the synagogues and the head table at banquets. Yet they shamelessly cheat widows out of their property and then pretend to be pious by making long prayers in public. Because of this, they will be more severely punished."

Jesus sat down near the collection box in the Temple and watched as the crowds dropped in their money. Many rich people put in large amounts. Then a poor widow came and dropped in two small coins. Jesus called His disciples to Him and said, "I tell you the truth, this poor widow has given more than all the others who are making contributions. For they gave a tiny part of their surplus, but she, poor as she is, has given everything she had to live on."

MATTHEW 22:34-45

THE MOST IMPORTANT COMMANDMENT

But when the Pharisees heard that He had silenced the Sadducees with His reply, they met together to question Him again. One of them, an expert in religious law, tried to trap Him with this question: "Teacher, which is the most important commandment in the law of Moses?"

Jesus replied, "'You must love the LORD your God with all your heart, all your soul, and all your mind.' This is the first and greatest commandment. A second is equally important: 'Love your neighbor as yourself.' The entire law and all the demands of the prophets are based on these two commandments."

Then, surrounded by the Pharisees, Jesus asked them a question: "What do you think about the Messiah? Whose son is He?"

They replied, "He is the son of David." Jesus responded, "Then why does David, speaking under the inspiration of the Spirit, call the Messiah 'my Lord'? For David said, 'The LORD said to my Lord, Sit in the place of honor at My right hand until I humble your enemies beneath your feet.' Since David called the Messiah 'my Lord,' how can the Messiah be his son?" No one could answer Him. And after that, no one dared to ask Him any more questions.

I distinctly remember a season in college when I felt that God was silent. I was struggling to hear Him, see Him, and speak to His promises in my life. I will never forget when I was talking with a friend who was really struggling and the Lord so sweetly spoke to my own heart. "Believe this for you," He whispered. I knew what He meant. The head knowledge was not the issue; it was the heart knowledge that felt so far away. How did I get the very truth I was sharing with my friend in front of me into my own heart? The ten inches between my head and my heart felt more like one hundred feet.

Sitting with Jesus the next morning, I took the time to write out all the tangible ways I knew Jesus loved me and why I loved Him. It didn't happen immediately, but slowly, I felt Him stir my heart again. I began to see Him in the midst of my difficulties once more. And do you know what is the beautiful truth about this sequence of events? It was the Lord's love for me that allowed me to even pursue Him. His love is the only key that opens the door for me to love Him back. It is the honor of our lives.

In both the Gospels of Mark and Matthew, we see that the religious teachers were trying to trap Jesus with questions, hoping they could stump Him by making Him prioritize one thing over another. However, without flinching, Jesus told them that the greatest commandment and the commandment that preserves everyone is to love God with all our hearts. Not when it's convenient, not when it's trendy, and not just when tragedy strikes and we need rescue. It is our adoration of the Father that allows us to be love in action. Refreshment is found in the heart knowledge that He is life.

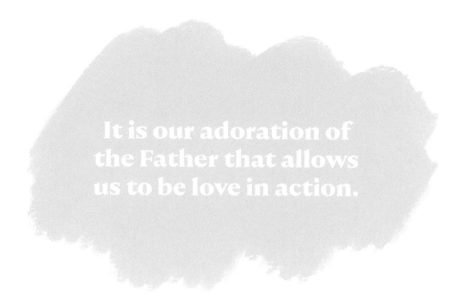

It is our adoration of
the Father that allows
us to be love in action.

1. *Do you struggle more in areas where you are having a hard time believing what God says about those particular areas? How can you change your thinking?*

2. *What does it mean to really "love God with all your heart"?*

3. *Only you know what goes on in your heart and mind. Do you think you are loving God with your life and decisions right now? How do you know?*

4. *When the teacher responded to Jesus with his head knowledge, Jesus replied, "You are not far from the Kingdom of God." What do you infer from this portion of the story?*

5. *In the version from Mark, Jesus says, "And how they love the seats of honor in the synagogues and the head table at banquets. Yet they shamelessly cheat widows out of their property and then pretend to be pious by making long prayers in public." Do you think religion often becomes the very thing that keeps us from loving God in our everyday lives? Explain.*

Dear Lord, thank You for this reminder that is sometimes hard to receive, yet receiving is the gateway to all things good and holy for our lives. How often we say that we love You and do the opposite of what You instruct! How quick we are to consume information for the sake of religion and not implement what it says so that it transforms our lives! Help us, Father.

Will You inspire in us a longing to dig into Your Word and ask the hard questions? Remove the pressure that we feel to be a super Christian, and alert us of any time when we begin to perform for our faith. We don't want to be impressive with our head knowledge; we want to be transformed by our heart knowledge. Identify in our lives anything that must change so that we can run hard after You.

Thank You for forgiving us quickly as we spend time wondering if Your love is enough. It is deep enough to cover any grievance, wide enough to cover all our mistakes, and high enough to allow us to be citizens of heaven. I want to approach this day with deeper hunger. Help me not be satisfied with a lukewarm life or a life that talks about my faith when I am not living to advance Your kingdom.

We get to love You because You first loved us. It is the greatest and most glorious mystery.

In the unconditional and relentless name of Jesus, amen.

MEDITATE ON HIS LOVE

DEUTERONOMY 6:5 ESV

You shall love the Lord your God with all your heart and with all your soul and with all your might.

I JOHN 4:7 ESV

Beloved, let us love one another, for love is from God, and whoever loves has been born of God and knows God.

PROVERBS 3:5 ESV

Trust in the Lord with all your heart, and do not lean on your own understanding.

JOHN 14:23 ESV

Jesus answered him, "If anyone loves me, he will keep my word, and my Father will love him, and we will come to him and make our home with him.

PROVERBS 27:19 ESV

As in water face reflects face, so the heart of man reflects the man.

LEARN ABOUT HIS LOVE:

Created for Righteousness

MATTHEW 5:1–30; 38–48 NIV

Now when Jesus saw the crowds, He went up on a mountainside and sat down. His disciples came to Him, and He began to teach them.

THE BEATITUDES

He said:

"Blessed are the poor in spirit, for theirs is the kingdom of heaven.
Blessed are those who mourn, for they will be comforted.
Blessed are the meek, for they will inherit the earth.
Blessed are those who hunger and thirst for righteousness, for they will be filled.
Blessed are the merciful, for they will be shown mercy.
Blessed are the pure in heart, for they will see God.
Blessed are the peacemakers, for they will be called children of God.
Blessed are those who are persecuted because of righteousness, for theirs is the kingdom of heaven.

"Blessed are you when people insult you, persecute you and falsely say all kinds of evil against you because of Me. Rejoice and be glad, because great is your reward in heaven, for in the same way they persecuted the prophets who were before you. You are the salt of the earth. But if the salt loses its saltiness, how can it be made salty again? It is no longer good for anything, except to be thrown out and trampled underfoot.

"You are the light of the world. A town built on a hill cannot be hidden. Neither do people light a lamp and put it under a bowl. Instead they put it on its stand, and it gives light to everyone in the house. In the same way, let your light shine before others, that they may see your good deeds and glorify your Father in heaven.

"Do not think that I have come to abolish the Law or the Prophets; I have not come to abolish them but to fulfill them. For truly I tell you, until heaven and earth disappear, not the smallest letter, not the least stroke of a pen, will by any means disappear from the Law until everything is accomplished. Therefore anyone who sets aside one of the least of these commands and teaches others accordingly will be called least in the kingdom of heaven, but whoever practices and teaches

these commands will be called great in the kingdom of heaven. For I tell you that unless your righteousness surpasses that of the Pharisees and the teachers of the law, you will certainly not enter the kingdom of heaven.

"You have heard that it was said to the people long ago, 'You shall not murder, and anyone who murders will be subject to judgment.' But I tell you that anyone who is angry with a brother or sister will be subject to judgment. Again, anyone who says to a brother or sister, 'Raca,' is answerable to the court. And anyone who says, 'You fool!' will be in danger of the fire of hell.

"Therefore, if you are offering your gift at the altar and there remember that your brother or sister has something against you, leave your gift there in front of the altar. First go and be reconciled to them; then come and offer your gift.

"Settle matters quickly with your adversary who is taking you to court. Do it while you are still together on the way, or your adversary may hand you over to the judge, and the judge may hand you over to the officer, and you may be thrown into prison. Truly I tell you, you will not get out until you have paid the last penny.

"You have heard that it was said, 'You shall not commit adultery.' But I tell you that anyone who looks at a woman lustfully has already committed adultery with her in his heart. If your right eye causes you to stumble, gouge it out and throw it away. It is better for you to lose one part of your body than for your whole body to be thrown into hell. And if your right hand causes you to stumble, cut it off and throw it away. It is better for you to lose one part of your body than for your whole body to go into hell.". . .

EYE FOR EYE

"You have heard that it was said, 'Eye for eye, and tooth for tooth.' But I tell you, do not resist an evil person. If anyone slaps you on the right cheek, turn to them the other cheek also. And if anyone wants to sue you and take your shirt, hand over your coat as well. If anyone forces you to go one mile, go with them two miles. Give to the one who asks you, and do not turn away from the one who wants to borrow from you.

"You have heard that it was said, 'Love your neighbor and hate your enemy.' But I tell you, love your enemies and pray for those who persecute you, that you may be children of your Father in heaven. He causes His sun to rise on the evil and the good, and sends rain on the righteous and the unrighteous. If you love those who love you, what reward will you get? Are not even the tax collectors doing that? And if you greet only your own people, what are you doing more than others? Do not even pagans do that? Be perfect, therefore, as your heavenly Father is perfect."

If we were to ask, "How does Jesus want me to act?" this passage—the Sermon on the Mount—would provide a great example. All of these attitudes and characteristics are things we are given as citizens of heaven, and are also markers for the people we'd like to be. These Scriptures are not merely a list of TO-DO and NOT TO-DO, dragging people down in bondage. They are encouragement for the heart and nourishment for the soul that speak to the deepest parts of us.

If Jesus were a coach (roll with me for the sake of the analogy), then I imagine this would be His locker room speech. How does a coach instigate a total turn-around for his players when they return to the game? He reminds them of who they are deep down, the champions that they were created to be, why they put on that jersey in the first place, and who they are called to be. He knows that the work of their hands and the pursuit of excellence are always fueled by what is happening within them.

In my own life, sometimes I attach my value to the worldly success I achieve, knowing that it will never satisfy. This can quickly turn the Sermon on the Mount from life-changing to life-condemning. But, amidst my striving, I can hear Jesus whisper, "You will never find satisfaction drinking from that well." Why drink from the well of performance when the well of purpose is so close by? Because you and I? We were created for righteousness—we are cities on a hill and the salt of the earth. May our thirst for righteousness be extreme, knowing earth will soon fade and heaven is coming.

We were created
for righteousness—
we are cities on a hill and
the salt of the earth.

1. *Look at the beginning "blesseds" in the Bible verse. Is there a particular "blessed" with which you identify?*

2. *What does it mean to be a peacemaker in your personal life?*

3. When you read through the Sermon on the Mount, does it make you feel ashamed or convicted? Why or why not? Remember, Jesus came to fulfill the law but also to help us pursue righteousness in grace. Don't hold on to feelings of guilt or shame! Give it all to Him.

4. Imagine being a disciple sitting with Jesus on this mountain and listening to this sermon. How do you think you would feel?

5. It is obvious that Jesus talks with authority as He preaches, not asking for affirmation in His instruction. Does the tone of His authority help you receive what He is saying as true? Why or why not?

Dear Lord, thinking about You preaching this sermon on the mountain with Your disciples never ceases to amaze me. Throughout Your Word You often stop and make time for Your people. No shortcuts, no CliffsNotes, no abridged versions of truth—You always have their best in mind.

I know I was created to pursue righteousness and keep heaven always on my mind. Sometimes I fall into the trap of being a victim of my own thoughts or feeling the pressure to conform based on what is around me. But Jesus, You always offer a different way. Your way brings blessing and promise, hope and peace.

Though I know it may be painful and will require me to strip off what entangles me, will You lead me in pursuing holiness? From the little to the big, help me reflect Your heart.

When it comes to the people in my life, help me be quick to forgive and generous with all that I have.

When it comes to the posture of my heart, show me how to be a peacemaker and pure in spirit.

When it comes to the position of my treasure, plant me deep in the truth of Your Word.

I do not have to chase happiness; when I run after You, I will find it. You are refining and cleansing me from the inside out. The narrow way is what I choose.

In the righteous and authoritative name of Jesus, amen.

MEDITATE ON HIS LOVE

II CORINTHIANS 5:21 ESV

For our sake he made him to be sin who knew no sin, so that in him we might become the righteousness of God.

ROMANS 15:5 NASB

Now may the God who gives perseverance and encouragement grant you to be of the same mind with one another, according to Christ Jesus.

I PETER 4:1 NIV

Therefore, since Christ suffered in His body, arm yourselves also with the same attitude, because whoever suffers in the body is done with sin.

ROMANS 12:16 NIV

Live in harmony with one another. Do not be proud, but be willing to associate with people of low position. Do not be conceited.

PHILIPPIANS 1:27 NIV

Whatever happens, conduct yourselves in a manner worthy of the gospel of Christ. Then, whether I come and see you or only hear about you in my absence, I will know that you stand firm in the one Spirit, striving together as one for the faith of the gospel.

For more on this topic, scan the QR code for a video message from Cleere.

LEARN ABOUT HIS LOVE

Forgiven without Finding Fault

LUKE 15:1–32 NLT

Tax collectors and other notorious sinners often came to listen to Jesus teach. This made the Pharisees and teachers of religious law complain that He was associating with such sinful people—even eating with them!

So Jesus told them this story: "If a man has a hundred sheep and one of them gets lost, what will he do? Won't he leave the ninety-nine others in the wilderness and go to search for the one that is lost until he finds it? And when he has found it, he will joyfully carry it home on his shoulders. When he arrives, he will call together his friends and neighbors, saying, 'Rejoice with me because I have found my lost sheep.' In the same way, there is more joy in heaven over one lost sinner who repents and returns to God than over ninety-nine others who are righteous and haven't strayed away!

PARABLE OF THE LOST COIN

"Or suppose a woman has ten silver coins and loses one. Won't she light a lamp and sweep the entire house and search carefully until she finds it? And when she finds it, she will call in her friends and neighbors and say, 'Rejoice with me because I have found my lost coin.' In the same way, there is joy in the presence of

God's angels when even one sinner repents."

PARABLE OF THE LOST SON

To illustrate the point further, Jesus told them this story: "A man had two sons. The younger son told his father, 'I want my share of your estate now before you die.' So his father agreed to divide his wealth between his sons.

"A few days later this younger son packed all his belongings and moved to a distant land, and there he wasted all his money in wild living. About the time his money ran out, a great famine swept over the land, and he began to starve. He persuaded a local farmer to hire him, and the man sent him into his fields to feed the pigs. The young man became so hungry that even the pods he was feeding the pigs looked good to him. But no one gave him anything.

"When he finally came to his senses, he said to himself, 'At home even the hired servants have food enough to spare, and here I am dying of hunger! I will go home to my father and say, "Father, I have sinned against both heaven and you, and I am no longer worthy of being called your son. Please take me on as a hired servant."'

"So he returned home to his father. And while he was still a long way off, his father saw him coming. Filled with love and compassion, he ran to his son, embraced him, and kissed him. His son said to him, 'Father, I have sinned against both heaven and you, and I am no longer worthy of being called your son.'

"But his father said to the servants, 'Quick! Bring the finest robe in the house and put it on him. Get a ring for his finger and sandals for his feet. And kill the calf we have been fattening. We must celebrate with a feast, for this son of mine was dead and has now returned to life. He was lost, but now he is found.' So the party began.

"Meanwhile, the older son was in the fields working. When he returned home, he heard music and dancing in the house, and he asked one of the servants what was going on. 'Your brother is back,' he was told, 'and your father has killed the fattened calf. We are celebrating because of his safe return.'

"The older brother was angry and wouldn't go in. His father came out and begged him, but he replied, 'All these years I've slaved for you and never once refused to do a single thing you told me to. And in all that time you never gave me even one young goat for a feast with my friends. Yet when this son of yours comes back after squandering your money on prostitutes, you celebrate by killing the fattened calf!'

"His father said to him, 'Look, dear son, you have always stayed by me, and everything I have is yours. We had to celebrate this happy day. For your brother was dead and has come back to life! He was lost, but now he is found!'"

So many things come to mind when reading this story: joy, gratitude, relief, peace, freedom, hope, strength, grace. It is truly a picture of the gospel. I feel like we all can relate to the prodigal son, more than we would like to admit, squandering what is given to us and thinking we can find better in the world "out there" than we can in the place God has us. Frantically searching for belonging but letting our pride take the lead, we follow what feels good, despite our Father's instructions, and we end up disappointed, discouraged, and dissatisfied.

I have a very distinct memory from my teenage years when I knew I was doing wrong. That conviction was made obvious by my desire to hide my actions, which then led to shame. I thought I was doing an incredible job of keeping it from my parents; little did I know, they were giving me the freedom to learn on my own and praying that I'd turn around and run back home. I remember the day I decided I was going to actually get honest with myself, and therefore others. Despite the thick cloud of shame that wanted to smother me, I could feel my heavenly Father's touch. His relentless love had been pursuing me, and my exhaustion finally allowed me to receive it. Why was I so convinced I couldn't turn around?

I love the honesty and reality of Scripture. We have all been the prodigal son and Jesus is always the Father, looking for us while we are still a long way off, never ever giving up anticipating our return to His front porch. Praise God for this truth.

Despite the thick cloud of shame that wanted to smother me, I could feel my heavenly Father's touch.

PONDER HIS LOVE

1. *Scripture says that tax collectors and notorious sinners came to hear Jesus preach. Why do you think they came to Him?*

2. *When it talks about heaven celebrating more over the lost sinner repenting than the righteous continuing on their path, what does that tell you about the character of God and the atmosphere of heaven? Does it make you view your own mistakes differently?*

3. Scripture says, "And while he was still a long way off, his father saw him coming." How has Jesus' love reached you, even in the most distant of places?

4. The older brother was angry and jealous that his brother was receiving such a celebration instead of consequences. Can you see yourself in this situation at all? When have you found it frustrating when good things happened for those you didn't believe deserved it?

5. Looking at the relationships in your life, how can you create time in your schedule or room in your heart to pursue the lost or hurting?

Dear Lord, thank You for these stories of the lost sheep, the lost coin, and the prodigal son. I want to read them over and over again, overwhelmed at how You leave the ninety-nine and pursue the one. That is not just a tagline, that is Your heart. Knowing that I have been the one you have searched for and rescued in the past makes me sad that I would ever run away from such a loving and compassionate Father.

Lord, I see myself in the prodigal son in so many ways. I'm sorry for the times I have asked for my inheritance before it was time, trusting my hands to know how to better steward my future than Yours do. Forge in me a repentant heart any time that I stray from Your Word or doubt who You are. Your love is reckless, unconditional, and relentless—help me lean into it, not try to earn it or run from it. No shame, no fear, just full belief that my Father's arms embrace all that I am and all that I bring home.

Will You break any part of my flesh that responds like the older brother toward others in my life? You are just and You are generous. I want to celebrate everything that moves Your kingdom forward and helps Your people break free.

Thank You for such crazy love. You are the Father with a heart for the prodigal and I am forever grateful.

In the forgiving and unconditionally loving name of Jesus, amen.

MEDITATE ON HIS LOVE

JAMES 1:5 NIV

If any of you lacks wisdom, you should ask God, who gives generously to all without finding fault, and it will be given to you

EPHESIANS 4:30–32 NIV

Do not grieve the Holy Spirit of God, with whom you were sealed for the day of redemption. Get rid of all bitterness, rage and anger, brawling and slander, along with every form of malice. Be kind and compassionate to one another, forgiving each other, just as in Christ God forgave you.

ISAIAH 54:10 ESV

"For the mountains may depart and the hills be removed, but my steadfast love shall not depart from you, and my covenant of peace shall not be removed," says the LORD, who has compassion on you.

ACTS 3:19 NIV

Repent, then, and turn to God, so that your sins may be wiped out, that times of refreshing may come from the Lord.

II CHRONICLES 30:9 NIV

The LORD your God is gracious and compassionate. He will not turn His face from you if you return to him.

LEARN FROM HIS LOVE

Redefined by Favor

I SAMUEL 18:1-30 NLT

After David had finished talking with Saul, he met Jonathan, the king's son. There was an immediate bond between them, for Jonathan loved David. From that day on Saul kept David with him and wouldn't let him return home. And Jonathan made a solemn pact with David, because he loved him as he loved himself. Jonathan sealed the pact by taking off his robe and giving it to David, together with his tunic, sword, bow, and belt.

Whatever Saul asked David to do, David did it successfully. So Saul made him a commander over the men of war, an appointment that was welcomed by the people and Saul's officers alike.

When the victorious Israelite army was returning home after David had killed the Philistine, women from all the towns of Israel came out to meet King Saul. They sang and danced for joy with tambourines and cymbals. This was their song: "Saul has killed his thousands, and David his ten thousands!"

This made Saul very angry. "What's this?" he said. "They credit David with ten thousands and me with only thousands. Next they'll be making him their king!" So from that time on Saul kept a jealous eye on David.

The very next day a tormenting spirit from God overwhelmed Saul, and he began to rave in his house like a madman. David was playing the harp, as he did each day. But Saul had a spear in his hand, and he suddenly hurled it at David, intending to pin him to the wall. But David escaped him twice.

Saul was then afraid of David, for the LORD was with David and had turned away from Saul. Finally, Saul sent him away and appointed him commander over 1,000 men, and David faithfully led his troops into battle.

David continued to succeed in everything he did, for the LORD was with him. When Saul recognized this, he became even more afraid of him. But all Israel and Judah loved David because he was so successful at leading his troops into battle.

DAVID MARRIES SAUL'S DAUGHTER

One day Saul said to David, "I am ready to give you my older daughter, Merab, as your wife. But first you must prove yourself to be a real warrior by fighting the LORD's battles." For Saul thought, "I'll send him out against the Philistines and let them kill him rather than doing it myself."

"Who am I, and what is my family in Israel that I should be the king's son-in-law?" David exclaimed. "My father's family is nothing!" So when the time came for Saul to give his daughter Merab in marriage to David, he gave her instead to Adriel, a man from Meholah.

In the meantime, Saul's daughter Michal had fallen in love with David, and Saul was delighted when he heard about it. "Here's another chance to see him killed by the Philistines!" Saul said to himself. But to David he said, "Today you have a second chance to become my son-in-law!"

Then Saul told his men to say to David, "The king really likes you, and so do we. Why don't you accept the king's offer and become his son-in-law?" When Saul's men said these things to David, he replied, "How can a poor man from a humble family afford the bride price for the daughter of a king?"

When Saul's men reported this back to the king, he told them, "Tell David that all I want for the bride price is 100 Philistine foreskins! Vengeance on my enemies is all I really want." But what Saul had in mind was that David would be killed in the fight.

David was delighted to accept the offer. Before the time limit expired, he and his men went out and killed 200 Philistines. Then David fulfilled the king's requirement by presenting all their foreskins to him. So Saul gave his daughter Michal to David to be his wife. When Saul realized that the LORD was with David and how much his daughter Michal loved him, Saul became even more afraid of him, and he remained David's enemy for the rest of his life.

Every time the commanders of the Philistines attacked, David was more successful against them than all the rest of Saul's officers. So David's name became very famous.

David was a man who was continually positioned in challenging situations: fighting Goliath, becoming commander over the Israelite army, earning the right to marry the king's daughter, and then Saul's continued hatred. However, time after time after time, David shows up, humbles himself, and walks in the confidence that God is with him and for him.

This story really challenged my heart more than my mind. My mind and my mouth declare that God's favor is upon me because I am His child; however, does my heart really believe it? Because if so, like David, my belief changes my approach to battle, my willingness to do the hard things, and how much I value what others say about me. I would like to think that I would keep fighting and keep persevering like David, despite what King Saul said about me. However, the people-pleasing side of me is blown away by David's firm stance in such a grace-giving way.

The story ends by telling us of David's continued success in the kingdom. How encouraging is that? Despite everything, the favor of God prevailed and allowed him to be resilient. May we nestle ourselves so deep in the Word of God and trust His character that, like David, we become examples to a watching world that God's favor is the greatest gift of our lives.

> May we nestle ourselves so
> deep in the Word of God and
> trust His character that, like
> David, we become examples to a
> watching world that God's favor
> is the greatest gift of our lives.

PONDER HIS LOVE

1. *Though Jonathan was the king's son and a little older than David, he humbled himself and made a pact with David to fully support David becoming king. Do you think you are a Jonathan kind of friend to others or does your pride tend to lead your relationships? Explain.*

2. *David conquered the Philistines, escaped danger, and found favor in all situations. Does it seem hard to believe that the favor of God is this strong? Why or why not?*

3. *Saul became so jealous of David that his jealousy began to torment his spirit and distract him from everyday life. Describe a pattern you've seen in your life when you have been jealous or frustrated. How do you overcome this pattern?*

4. *Scripture says, "Saul became even more afraid of him, and he remained David's enemy for the rest of his life." How do you combat fear?*

5. *When you think of the "favor of God," what comes to your mind? How have you seen that in your life lately?*

Dear Lord, thank You for the person of David and his example of what it looks like to have a heart for You. Though we know that David was successful, it was not without a fight and great perseverance that he stayed the course. Will You help us remember this as we reflect on our own experiences and receive Your favor in the place we are today?

Posture our hearts so that we look for the light in all situations, knowing that there is nowhere we can go that Your presence is not found. Help us be people who initiate action and move forward based on the truth that we already know about You and Your promises. Our lives are built on the covenant You made with us long ago; we can find hope and courage because of this gift.

Show us how to redefine what Your favor looks like in our lives. It doesn't equate with easy or perfect; rather, it is us showing up, using our gifts, giving our all, and trusting that You will guide and lead where You see fit. And when challenges arise that confront our pride or make us question our stability, remind us that You are also in this place. Help us see every bit of opposition as a way to become stronger, and activate our faith in a world that is so desperately looking for the real thing. Your kindness, love, and peace bring favor to our hearts. We are grateful.

In the radiant and generous name of Jesus, amen.

MEDITATE ON HIS LOVE

PSALM 5:12 ESV

For You bless the righteous, O Lord; you cover him with favor as with a shield.

PSALM 30:5 ESV

For his anger is but for a moment, and his favor is for a lifetime. Weeping may tarry for the night, but joy comes with the morning.

PROVERBS 3:1-4 ESV

My son, do not forget my teaching, but let your heart keep my commandments, for length of days and years of life and peace they will add to you. Let not steadfast love and faithfulness forsake you; bind them around your neck; write them on the tablet of your heart. So you will find favor and good success in the sight of God and man.

EXODUS 33:17 ESV

The Lord said to Moses, "This very thing that you have spoken I will do, for you have found favor in my sight, and I know you by name."

NUMBERS 6:25-26 ESV

The Lord make his face to shine upon you and be gracious to you; the Lord lift up his countenance upon you and give you peace.

LEARN ABOUT HIS LOVE

Committed to Love

RUTH 1–2:7 NLT

In the days when the judges ruled in Israel, a severe famine came upon the land. So a man from Bethlehem in Judah left his home and went to live in the country of Moab, taking his wife and two sons with him. The man's name was Elimelech, and his wife was Naomi. Their two sons were Mahlon and Kilion. They were Ephrathites from Bethlehem in the land of Judah. And when they reached Moab, they settled there.

Then Elimelech died, and Naomi was left with her two sons. The two sons married Moabite women. One married a woman named Orpah, and the other a woman named Ruth. But about ten years later, both Mahlon and Kilion died. This left Naomi alone, without her two sons or her husband.

NAOMI AND RUTH RETURN

Then Naomi heard in Moab that the LORD had blessed his people in Judah by giving them good crops again. So Naomi and her daughters-in-law got ready to leave Moab to return to her homeland. With her two daughters-in-law she set out from the place where she had been living, and they took the road that would lead them back to Judah.

But on the way, Naomi said to her two daughters-in-law, "Go back to your mothers' homes. And may the LORD reward you for your kindness to your husbands and to me. May the Lord bless you with the security of another marriage." Then she kissed them good-bye, and they all broke down and wept.

"No," they said. "We want to go with you to your people."

But Naomi replied, "Why should you go on with me? Can I still give birth to other sons who could grow up to be your husbands? No, my daughters, return to your parents' homes, for I am too old to marry again. And even if it were possible, and I were to get married tonight and bear sons, then what? Would you wait for them to grow up and refuse to marry someone else? No, of course not, my daughters! Things are far more bitter for me than for you, because the LORD himself has raised his fist against me."

And again they wept together, and Orpah kissed her mother-in-law good-bye. But Ruth clung tightly to Naomi. "Look," Naomi said to her, "your sister-in-law has gone back to her people and to her gods. You should do the same."

But Ruth replied, "Don't ask me to leave you and turn back. Wherever you go, I will go; wherever you live, I will live. Your people will be my people, and your God will be my God. Wherever you die, I will die, and there I will be buried. May the LORD punish me severely if I allow anything but death to separate us!" When Naomi saw that Ruth was determined to go with her, she said nothing more.

So the two of them continued on their journey. When they came to Bethlehem, the entire town was excited by their arrival. "Is it really Naomi?" the women asked.

"Don't call me Naomi," she responded. "Instead, call me Mara, for the Almighty has made life very bitter for me. I went away full, but the LORD has brought me home empty. Why call me Naomi when the LORD has caused me to suffer and the Almighty has sent such tragedy upon me?"

So Naomi returned from Moab, accompanied by her daughter-in-law Ruth, the young Moabite woman. They arrived in Bethlehem in late spring, at the beginning of the barley harvest.

RUTH WORKS IN BOAZ'S FIELD

Now there was a wealthy and influential man in Bethlehem named Boaz, who was a relative of Naomi's husband, Elimelech.

One day Ruth the Moabite said to Naomi, "Let me go out into the harvest fields to pick up the stalks of grain left behind by anyone who is kind enough to let me do it."

Naomi replied, "All right, my daughter, go ahead." So Ruth went out to gather grain behind the harvesters. And as it happened, she found herself working in a field that belonged to Boaz, the relative of her father-in-law, Elimelech.

While she was there, Boaz arrived from Bethlehem and greeted the harvesters. "The LORD be with you!" he said.

"The LORD bless you!" the harvesters replied.

Then Boaz asked his foreman, "Who is that young woman over there? Who does she belong to?"

And the foreman replied, "She is the young woman from Moab who came back with Naomi. She asked me this morning if she could gather grain behind the harvesters. She has been hard at work ever since, except for a few minutes' rest in the shelter."

We can all relate to the pull of family ties, right? Sometimes it's good, and other times, it's really difficult to navigate. I love the humanity of Naomi and Ruth in this story. We read about their sadness as they weep when Naomi does her best to send away both of her daughters-in-law to find better lives. Naomi is honest about her state of bitterness and the hardness of her heart. And then we see Ruth's reaction, hearing the fight in her words and her unwavering commitment to her mother-in-law despite the fact that she was a struggling widow.

I put myself in this position and I wonder, *Would I have been Ruth or Orpah?* Naomi gave both women full permission to leave, knowing that their lives were no longer the joyous, fulfilling ones they had signed up for when they married her sons. Orpah goes her own way and Ruth clings to Naomi. Her commitment is no longer based on circumstances or preference, but on her desire to please God and serve Him first and foremost. I believe Ruth's empathy and compassion for Naomi were heaven sent, allowing her to remain in the hard times so that she could point to the holiness of her heavenly Father.

Thinking about God's commitment to us is overwhelming. Though Ruth is a strong example, there is no one and nothing that can adequately convey the covenant promise our heavenly Father has made toward us. Our bad moods, betrayal, bitterness about our circumstances, and even our blatant rejection of Him don't make Him second-guess whether He will stay. Now that should comfort the deepest part of our souls.

There is no one and nothing
that can adequately convey the
covenant promise our heavenly
Father has made toward us.

1. *Naomi felt as though God had raised His fist at her since her life had been turned upside down. Can you relate to this feeling? How do you keep from being bitter?*

2. *Family ties are often the most tested of all our relationships. When have yours been tested and how did you see God in that circumstance?*

3.   *When has the gift of a committed friendship helped you discover something about yourself and about God?*

4.   *Ruth was not dealt the best hand at first. However, her commitment to Naomi and her hard-working efforts in the field earned the attention of Boaz, who later made her his wife. When have you seen how resilience amidst the most difficult times provides deeper connections to those around you?*

5.   *Do you find it hard to believe that God's commitment to His people is not based on anything that they've done? Why?*

Dear Lord, thank You for this vulnerable and comforting story of commitment between Ruth and Naomi. It challenges my soul and comforts my heart.

To be honest, I can easily see myself in Orpah. It's so easy to let my flesh lead the way and forget my commitments, especially when they become hard. But Jesus, I desire to look like You and follow in the way of Ruth. She was not looking for an escape route or for the easy way. She knew a hard road was ahead and she chose to stay on it. Will You help me stay the course? Help me discern my commitments so that I can firmly walk in them.

Thank You for the way You provide people in our lives to link arms with and help us see the light when it seems so dim. Like Naomi, I can feel my fragility and vulnerability, and I want to send people away from it. It feels heavy and burdensome; however, this is the point of community. Help me voice my needs and be willing to break when others are watching. Even when I feel as though You don't hear me, this story reminds me that You are always listening and advocating for my life.

Thank You for people like Ruth and Boaz who are aware of the needs of others and humble themselves before responding. Open my eyes and make me alert. Help me look for those who are breaking and hurting. Show me how to hold their arms up, stand in the gap, and speak life into the place where they are walking.

In the unwavering and unconditional love of Jesus, amen.

MEDITATE ON HIS LOVE

LUKE 9:62 NIV

Jesus replied, "No one who puts a hand to the plow and looks back is fit for service in the kingdom of God."

PROVERBS 16:3 NIV

Commit to the LORD whatever you do, and He will establish your plans.

ROMANS 8:38–39 NKJV

For I am persuaded that neither death nor life, nor angels nor principalities nor powers, nor things present nor things to come, nor height nor depth, nor any other created thing, shall be able to separate us from the love of God which is in Christ Jesus our Lord.

PSALM 94:14 NKJV

The LORD will not cast off His people, nor will He forsake His inheritance.

EXODUS 19:5 NASB

Now then, if you will indeed obey My voice and keep My covenant, then you shall be My own possession among all the peoples, for all the earth is Mine.

LEARN ABOUT HIS LOVE

Compelled by Courage

ESTHER 7-8 NLT

So the king and Haman went to Queen Esther's banquet. On this second occasion, while they were drinking wine, the king again said to Esther, "Tell me what you want, Queen Esther. What is your request? I will give it to you, even if it is half the kingdom!"

Queen Esther replied, "If I have found favor with the king, and if it pleases the king to grant my request, I ask that my life and the lives of my people will be spared. For my people and I have been sold to those who would kill, slaughter, and annihilate us. If we had merely been sold as slaves, I could remain quiet, for that would be too trivial a matter to warrant disturbing the king."

"Who would do such a thing?" King Xerxes demanded. "Who would be so presumptuous as to touch you?"

Esther replied, "This wicked Haman is our adversary and our enemy." Haman grew pale with fright before the king and queen. Then the king jumped to his feet in a rage and went out into the palace garden.

Haman, however, stayed behind to plead for his life with Queen Esther, for he knew that the king intended to kill him. In despair he fell on the couch where Queen Esther was reclining, just as the king was returning from the palace garden.

The king exclaimed, "Will he even assault the queen right here in the palace, before my very eyes?" And as soon as the king spoke, his attendants covered Haman's face, signaling his doom.

Then Harbona, one of the king's eunuchs, said, "Haman has set up a sharpened pole that stands seventy-five feet tall in his own courtyard. He intended to use it to impale Mordecai, the man who saved the king from assassination."

"Then impale Haman on it!" the king ordered. So they impaled Haman on the pole he had set up for Mordecai, and the king's anger subsided.

A DECREE TO HELP THE JEWS

On that same day King Xerxes gave the property of Haman, the enemy of the Jews, to Queen Esther. Then Mordecai was brought before the king, for Esther had told the king how they were related. The king took off his signet ring—which he had taken back from Haman—and gave it to Mordecai. And Esther appointed Mordecai to be in charge of Haman's property.

Then Esther went again before the king, falling down at his feet and begging him with tears to stop the evil plot devised by Haman the Agagite against the Jews. Again the king held out the gold scepter to Esther. So she rose and stood before him.

Esther said, "If it please the king, and if I have found favor with him, and if he thinks it is right, and if I am pleasing to him, let there be a decree that reverses the orders of Haman son of Hammedatha the Agagite, who ordered that Jews throughout all the king's provinces should be destroyed. For how can I endure to see my people and my family slaughtered and destroyed?"

Then King Xerxes said to Queen Esther and Mordecai the Jew, "I have given Esther the property of Haman, and he has been impaled on a pole because he tried to destroy the Jews. Now go ahead and send a message to the Jews in the king's name, telling them whatever you want, and seal it with the king's signet ring. But remember that whatever has already been written in the king's name and sealed with his signet ring can never be revoked."

So on June 25 the king's secretaries were summoned, and a decree was written exactly as Mordecai dictated. It was sent to the Jews and to the highest officers, the governors, and the nobles of all the 127 provinces stretching from India to Ethiopia. The decree was written in the scripts and languages of all the peoples of the empire, including that of the Jews. The decree was written in the name of King Xerxes and sealed with the king's signet ring. Mordecai sent the dispatches by swift messengers, who rode fast horses especially bred for the king's service.

The king's decree gave the Jews in every city authority to unite to defend their lives. They were allowed to kill, slaughter, and annihilate anyone of any nationality or province who might attack them or their children and wives, and to take the property of their enemies. The day chosen for this event throughout all the provinces of King Xerxes was March 7 of the next year.

A copy of this decree was to be issued as law in every province and proclaimed to all peoples, so that the Jews would be ready to take revenge on their enemies on the appointed day. So urged on by the king's command, the messengers rode out swiftly on fast horses bred for the king's service. The same decree was also proclaimed in the fortress of Susa.

Then Mordecai left the king's presence, wearing the royal robe of blue and white, the great crown of gold, and an outer cloak of fine linen and purple. And the people of Susa celebrated the new decree. The Jews were filled with joy and gladness and were honored everywhere. In every province and city, wherever the king's decree arrived, the Jews rejoiced and had a great celebration and declared a public festival and holiday. And many of the people of the land became Jews themselves, for they feared what the Jews might do to them.

We see in the Bible that Esther was merely a Jewish girl who entered a beauty contest and sailed to the top, later to be selected as queen of Persia. King Xerxes throws a lavish banquet, and Haman's plot to annihilate the Jewish people is revealed. Esther speaks up and pleads with the king that if he could just grant her one request, it would be to save the Jewish people from the hands of Haman and his army. Mordecai, Esther's cousin, was keeping her briefed on what was happening outside the royal gates, and Haman had promised his death.

When reading this, I don't think I initially realized the risk that Esther was taking. Wasn't she queen? How was this a big deal? But we see all throughout Scripture that when the pride of a king and his people are threatened, the reactions are shocking and scary. Queen Esther never forgot her roots. I love that she recognized that it was possible that she became queen for exactly this reason—to rescue the Jewish population. She didn't let what made her stand apart from those in the palace make her shrink back; this became the source of her courage.

Esther's bravery was what turned the entire story upside down, changed Xerxes' mind, ended Haman's life, placed favor on Mordecai's life, and positioned the Jews to experience victory for years to come. I pray I am like Esther, letting the cries of God's people make me braver than my fears.

I pray I am like Esther, letting the cries of God's people make me braver than my fears.

PONDER HIS LOVE

1. *The book of Esther is the only book of the Bible that doesn't mention God. Where can you see His fingerprints and His sovereignty in this story?*

2. *Haman's pride was his pitfall; he desired personal power over everything. How have you seen your pride get in the way or cause destruction?*

3. We see that the king was volatile and emotionally all over the place. How did this play to Esther's advantage?

4. We see that the Jews immediately celebrated and rejoiced after their deliverance. How do you praise God when He has delivered you?

5. Is there a current situation in your life or a relationship where you know you must be brave? What are you scared of?

Dear Lord, thank You for this story of Esther and how You placed a young Jewish girl as the queen of a palace so that she could be a voice of justice and grace. It's easy to point the finger at Haman or King Xerxes and see their obvious fleshly tendencies and desire for personal gain; but Lord, I know my vision is often clouded by my own pride and desires. Will You convict my heart of any ways that I am letting my perspective be blurred? Help me remember that humility and fear of You are the foundation of all goodness.

Also, will You reveal to me the ways that You want me to be brave? Help me seek You in the place that I am and the position that You've put me in. I want to make much of heaven here. When courage feels far away, nudge me forward. My emotions may never align with the direction of obedience, but when I follow You, You infuse my spirit with the grace and strength to show up.

Your fingerprints are everywhere, even when my circumstances want to convince me that You're silent. Thank You for fighting to protect Your people. You have given me the armor that I need to enter the battle, fight anything that opposes Your truth, and to advance in the way of peace.

In the courageous and sovereign name of Jesus, amen.

MEDITATE ON HIS LOVE

PHILIPPIANS 1:28-29 NLT

Don't be intimidated in any way by your enemies. This will be a sign to them that they are going to be destroyed, but that you are going to be saved, even by God himself. For you have been given not only the privilege of trusting in Christ but also the privilege of suffering for Him.

ISAIAH 41:13 ESV

For I, the LORD your God, hold your right hand; it is I who say to you, "Fear not, I am the one who helps you."

EPHESIANS 4:1 ESV

I therefore, a prisoner for the Lord, urge you to walk in a manner worthy of the calling to which you have been called.

II TIMOTHY 1:7 ESV

For God gave us a spirit not of fear but of power and love and self-control.

PSALM 56:3-4 ESV

When I am afraid, I put my trust in you. In God, whose word I praise, in God I trust; I shall not be afraid. What can flesh do to me?

LEARN ABOUT HIS LOVE

Tested to Testify of His Love

LUKE 4:1-13; MATTHEW 4:1-11; MARK 1:12-13 NLT

LUKE 4:1-13

Then Jesus, full of the Holy Spirit, returned from the Jordan River. He was led by the Spirit in the wilderness, where He was tempted by the devil for forty days. Jesus ate nothing all that time and became very hungry.

Then the devil said to Him, "If you are the Son of God, tell this stone to become a loaf of bread."

But Jesus told him, "No! The Scriptures say, 'People do not live by bread alone.'"

Then the devil took Him up and revealed to Him all the kingdoms of the world in a moment of time. "I will give you the glory of these kingdoms and authority over them," the devil said, "because they are mine to give to anyone I please. I will give it all to You if you will worship me."

Jesus replied, "The Scriptures say,

> *'You must worship the LORD your God*
>   *and serve only Him.'"*

Then the devil took Him to Jerusalem, to the highest point of the Temple, and said, "If you are the Son of God, jump off! For the Scriptures say,

> *'He will order His angels to protect and guard you.*

> *And they will hold you up with their hands*
>   *so you won't even hurt your foot on a stone.'"*

Jesus responded, "The Scriptures also say, 'You must not test the LORD your God.'"

When the devil had finished tempting Jesus, he left Him until the next opportunity came.

MATTHEW 4:1-11

Then Jesus was led by the Spirit into the wilderness to be tempted there by the devil. For forty days and forty nights he fasted and became very hungry.

During that time the devil came and said to him, "If you are the Son of God, tell these stones to become loaves of bread."

But Jesus told him, "No! The Scriptures say,

> *'People do not live by bread alone,*
>   *but by every word that comes from*
>   *the mouth of God.'"*

Then the devil took him to the holy city, Jerusalem, to the highest point of the Temple, and said, "If you are the Son of God, jump off! For the Scriptures say,

'He will order his angels to protect you.
And they will hold you up with their hands
so you won't even hurt your foot on a stone.'"

Jesus responded, "The Scriptures also say, 'You must not test the Lord your God.'"

Next the devil took Him to the peak of a very high mountain and showed Him all the kingdoms of the world and their glory. "I will give it all to You," he said, "if You will kneel down and worship me."

"Get out of here, Satan," Jesus told him. "For the Scriptures say,

'You must worship the Lord your God
and serve only Him.'"

Then the devil went away, and angels came and took care of Jesus.

MARK 1:12-13

The Spirit then compelled Jesus to go into the wilderness, where he was tempted by Satan for forty days. He was out among the wild animals, and angels took care of Him.

I included all three versions of this story about Jesus in the wilderness because I think it is incredible to see how differently each Gospel describes it. Each version adds to our faith by allowing us to see it through three different lenses.

The first sentence alone made me come to a standstill. Wait a moment—the Spirit led Jesus into the wilderness? Obviously, the Spirit knew that Satan would be there to tempt Him and try to wear Him down, and yet He was led there anyway. The enemy tries to get at Jesus, knowing He is hungry and exhausted, by using the thing He knows the most: Scripture. However, Jesus is aware of His tactics and reaffirms His trust in His Father.

This challenged me, convicted me, and counseled me. Jesus was not surprised by opposition, and His obedience to the Spirit had nothing to do with His view or His preference. It had everything to do with His trust in God.

When I know I am in a wilderness season, I so easily want to run from God, blame Him, or allow my suffering to convince me that He doesn't see me or doesn't care. But if Jesus, the Son of God, was thrown into the wilderness, triggered by exhaustion, and tested by the enemy, why should I be surprised by opposition or the need for suffering?

I have seen in my own life, in every chapter that I didn't think I wanted in my story, that God was refining me in a way that only the wilderness can do. We can trust Him in the suffering; He is the only One who will sustain us there.

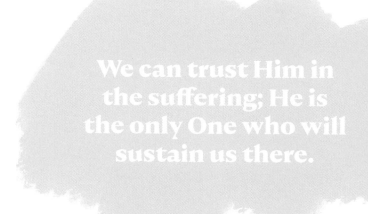

We can trust Him in the suffering; He is the only One who will sustain us there.

1. *Satan's first words to Jesus were, "If You are the son of God . . . Why do you think he attacks Jesus' identity first?*

2. *The enemy manipulates the Word of God to try and trap Jesus. Has he ever tried to take truth out of context in your life? How did you respond?*

3. *Jesus fasted for forty days while in the wilderness, forcing Him to depend on God and God alone in every way. When you have experienced a desert season, did you run toward or away from God?*

4. *Mark and Matthew both mention that angels came to take care of Jesus after the forty days were over and the testing was done. What does this reveal about God and His provision?*

5. *When you are in a hard season, what do you usually fear the most? How can you work to trust God more in that area?*

Dear Lord, thank You so much for including this story in three different Gospels; it reaffirms to my soul the importance and necessity of understanding Your heart in it. Reading it, I am so encouraged and challenged by Jesus. Even though I know the wilderness is crucial to my growth, I can feel my flesh already wanting to run at the sound of the word.

Sometimes I believe the lie that when I am being tested, I am doing something wrong or going the wrong way. Or I fear that the wilderness won't be just for a season and the hardness will permeate my life forever. But You, Lord, never leave me. Just as You did for Jesus, I know You will always equip me to fight any battle I face and send the enemy back where he belongs.

Will You elevate my perspective and help me recognize when I am exhausted so that I can be aware of the enemy's attacks? Realign my thoughts with the truth of Your Word. Show me how to cling to Your promises, even when I am weary.

Jesus used the time in the wilderness to fast and pray, not missing this opportunity to lean into Your stillness. Activate such radical faith in me, channeling my energy to seek You rather than outcomes or answers.

You are my Shepherd on the mountaintop and in the valley, in the wilderness and all the way to the Promised land.

In the faithful and trustworthy name of Jesus, amen.

MEDITATE ON HIS LOVE

DEUTERONOMY 29:5 ESV

I have led you forty years in the wilderness. Your clothes have not worn out on you, and your sandals have not worn out on your foot.

I CORINTHIANS 10:13 NLT

The temptations in your life are no different from what others experience. And God is faithful. He will not allow the temptation to be more than you can stand. When you are tempted, He will show you a way out so that you can endure.

PROVERBS 29:25 NLT

Fearing people is a dangerous trap, but trusting the LORD means safety.

I PETER 4:19 NLT

So if you are suffering in a manner that pleases God, keep on doing what is right, and trust your lives to the God who created you, for He will never fail you.

ZECHARIAH 13:9 NLT

I will bring that group through the fire and make them pure. I will refine them like silver and purify them like gold. They will call on My name, and I will answer them. I will say, "These are my people," and they will say, "The LORD is our God."

LEARN ABOUT HIS LOVE

Led by the Spirit

GALATIANS 5:4–6:10 NIV

You who are trying to be justified by the law have been alienated from Christ; you have fallen away from grace. For through the Spirit we eagerly await by faith the righteousness for which we hope. For in Christ Jesus neither circumcision nor uncircumcision has any value. The only thing that counts is faith expressing itself through love.

You were running a good race. Who cut in on you to keep you from obeying the truth? That kind of persuasion does not come from the one who calls you. "A little yeast works through the whole batch of dough." I am confident in the Lord that you will take no other view. The one who is throwing you into confusion, whoever that may be, will have to pay the penalty. Brothers and sisters, if I am still preaching circumcision, why am I still being persecuted? In that case the offense of the cross has been abolished. As for those agitators, I wish they would go the whole way and emasculate themselves!

LIFE BY THE SPIRIT

You, my brothers and sisters, were called to be free. But do not use your freedom to indulge the flesh; rather, serve one another humbly in love. For the entire law is fulfilled in keeping this one command: "Love your neighbor as yourself." If you bite and devour each other, watch out or you will be destroyed by each other.

So I say, walk by the Spirit, and you will not gratify the desires of the flesh. For the flesh desires what is contrary to the Spirit, and the Spirit what is contrary to the flesh. They are in conflict with each other, so that you are not to do whatever you want. But if you are led by the Spirit, you are not under the law.

The acts of the flesh are obvious: sexual immorality, impurity and debauchery; idolatry and witchcraft; hatred, discord, jealousy, fits of rage, selfish ambition, dissensions, factions and envy; drunkenness, orgies, and the like. I warn you, as I did before, that those who live like this will not inherit the kingdom of God.

But the fruit of the Spirit is love, joy, peace, forbearance, kindness, goodness, faithfulness, gentleness and self-control. Against such things there is no law. Those who belong to Christ Jesus have crucified the flesh with its passions and desires. Since we live by the Spirit, let us keep in step with the Spirit. Let us not become conceited, provoking and envying each other . . . .

Brothers and sisters, if someone is caught in a sin, you who live by the Spirit should restore that person gently. But watch yourselves, or you also may be tempted. Carry each other's burdens, and in this way you will fulfill the law of Christ. If anyone thinks they are something when they are not, they deceive themselves. Each one should test their own actions. Then they can take pride in themselves alone, without comparing themselves to someone else, for each one should carry their own load. Nevertheless, the one who receives instruction in the word should share all good things with their instructor.

Do not be deceived: God cannot be mocked. A man reaps what he sows. Whoever sows to please their flesh, from the flesh will reap destruction; whoever sows to please the Spirit, from the Spirit will reap eternal life. Let us not become weary in doing good, for at the proper time we will reap a harvest if we do not give up. Therefore, as we have opportunity, let us do good to all people, especially to those who belong to the family of believers.

How do we love others? By the Spirit. How do we offer patience when it's wearing thin? By the Spirit. How do we walk in kindness when we know it's not going to be reciprocated? By the Spirit. How do we choose joy and love and faithfulness and peace, even when our flesh wants to flare up? By the Spirit.

I will never forget the day I was driving to work and I received a text that rocked my world. It was unexpected and I knew it would change the course of my life. My stomach began to tie into knots as I started to reach into the jar of WORRIES + WHAT-IFS. Do you own one of those? It's not our friend. Anyway, as I pull into my office, the Holy Spirit clearly whispers to me, "You know, you don't have to open that jar anymore. You can talk to Me."

My situation didn't change, logistics still had to be dealt with, and there were still so many unknowns ahead, but I was reminded that because I have the Holy Spirit, I get to operate in a totally different manner. Refreshing myself in His presence and abiding in His truth, I was overwhelmed by the light. I realized very quickly that when I invited the Holy Spirit into my heart, that meant that I would choose His ways.

We are all used to opening the jar of WORRIES + WHAT-IFS, like a cookie jar that we don't even realize we open when we walk by. But how incredible that the Spirit provides a better way, a more loving way, a way that offers life. And it is always available.

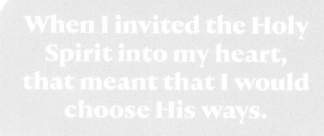

When I invited the Holy
Spirit into my heart,
that meant that I would
choose His ways.

1. *What is Paul's concern about our freedom? What does he say we will do with it?*

2. *When reading the list of the fruit of the Spirit, is there one that stands out that you struggle with? What about one that you easily offer/portray?*

3. *"The only thing that counts is faith expressing itself through love." What does that mean to you?*

4. *What does it mean to live by the Spirit? How does that change what you do and say?*

5. *Is there a certain practice or rhythm that you can implement to help you remember to always turn back to the Spirit?*

Dear Lord, thank You for the gift of the Holy Spirit and the way that You remind me of my responsibility to engage with Him in all that I do.

Even though I know my flesh is weak, I still expect myself to automatically respond in a way that pleases You. Will You help me practice operating in the Spirit, continually humbling my soul and remembering how often I forget?

Help me be alert to Your presence in the midst of my pain, Your sovereignty during the struggle, and Your faithfulness when I am fearful. I want to be a person that loves others well, meeting them right where they are and pointing them to You. Thank You for the supernatural ability You provide me to offer kindness, gentleness, and patience, even if it's not reciprocated or normal. It is in these moments that others learn about Your kingdom.

Refresh my soul as I sit with You. Coach my feet so that I walk in ways of righteousness. Examine my heart and unearth anything and everything that prevents intimacy with You.

Thank You for giving me the Spirit, who is louder than the chatter in my mind, the culture that pressures me, and the clutter that tries to envelop me.

The more I walk by the Spirit, the more I long to keep going. The more I walk by the Spirit, the better I love those around me. The more I walk by the Spirit, the greater I understand the meaning of a full and rich life. I'm so grateful.

In the Spirit-filled and abundant name of Jesus, amen.

MEDITATE ON HIS LOVE

EPHESIANS 5:2 ESV

Walk in love, as Christ loved us and gave himself up for us, a fragrant offering and sacrifice to God.

GALATIANS 2:20 ESV

I have been crucified with Christ. It is no longer I who live, but Christ who lives in me. And the life I now live in the flesh I live by faith in the Son of God, who loved me and gave himself for me.

ROMANS 8:5 ESV

For those who live according to the flesh set their minds on the things of the flesh, but those who live according to the Spirit set their minds on the things of the Spirit.

JOHN 6:63 ESV

It is the Spirit who gives life; the flesh is no help at all. The words that I have spoken to you are spirit and life.

II CORINTHIANS 5:5 ESV

He who has prepared us for this very thing is God, who has given us the Spirit as a guarantee.

For more on this topic, scan the QR code for a video message from Cleere.

LEARN ABOUT HIS LOVE

Called into Freedom

JOHN 4: 1–42 NLT

JESUS AND THE SAMARITAN WOMAN

Jesus knew the Pharisees had heard that He was baptizing and making more disciples than John (though Jesus Himself didn't baptize them—His disciples did). So He left Judea and returned to Galilee.

He had to go through Samaria on the way. Eventually He came to the Samaritan village of Sychar, near the field that Jacob gave to his son Joseph. Jacob's well was there; and Jesus, tired from the long walk, sat wearily beside the well about noontime. Soon a Samaritan woman came to draw water, and Jesus said to her, "Please give me a drink." He was alone at the time because His disciples had gone into the village to buy some food.

The woman was surprised, for Jews refuse to have anything to do with Samaritans. She said to Jesus, "You are a Jew, and I am a Samaritan woman. Why are you asking me for a drink?"

Jesus replied, "If you only knew the gift God has for you and who you are speaking to, you would ask Me, and I would give you living water."

"But sir, you don't have a rope or a bucket," she said, "and this well is very deep. Where would You get this living water? And besides, do You think You're greater than our ancestor Jacob, who gave us this well? How can You offer better water than he and his sons and his animals enjoyed?"

Jesus replied, "Anyone who drinks this water will soon become thirsty again. But those who drink the water I give will never be thirsty again. It becomes a fresh, bubbling spring within them, giving them eternal life."

"Please, sir," the woman said, "give me this water! Then I'll never be thirsty again, and I won't have to come here to get water."

"Go and get your husband," Jesus told her.

"I don't have a husband," the woman replied.

Jesus said, "You're right! You don't have a husband—for you have had five husbands, and you aren't even married to the man you're living with now. You certainly spoke the truth!"

"Sir," the woman said, "You must be a prophet. So tell me, why is it that you Jews insist that Jerusalem is the only place of worship, while we Samaritans claim it is here at Mount Gerizim, where our ancestors worshiped?"

Jesus replied, "Believe me, dear woman, the time is coming when it will no longer matter whether you worship the Father on this mountain or in Jerusalem. You Samaritans know very little about the one you worship, while we Jews know all about Him, for salvation comes through the Jews. But the time is coming—indeed it's here now—when true worshipers will worship the Father in spirit and in truth. The Father is looking for those who will worship Him that way. For God is Spirit, so those who worship Him must worship in spirit and in truth."

The woman said, "I know the Messiah is coming—the One who is called Christ. When He comes, He will explain everything to us."

Then Jesus told her, "I am the Messiah!"

Just then His disciples came back. They were shocked to find Him talking to a woman, but none of them had the nerve to ask, "What do you want with her?" or "Why are you talking to her?" The woman left her water jar beside the well and ran back to the village, telling everyone, "Come and see a man who told me everything I ever did! Could He possibly be the Messiah?" So the people came streaming from the village to see Him.

Meanwhile, the disciples were urging Jesus, "Rabbi, eat something."

But Jesus replied, "I have a kind of food you know nothing about."

"Did someone bring Him food while we were gone?" the disciples asked each other.

Then Jesus explained: "My nourishment comes from doing the will of God, who sent me, and from finishing His work. You know the saying, 'Four months between planting and harvest.' But I say, wake up and look around. The fields are already ripe for harvest. The harvesters are paid good wages, and the fruit they harvest is people brought to eternal life. What joy awaits both the planter and the harvester alike! You know the saying, 'One plants and another harvests.' And it's true. I sent you to harvest where you didn't plant; others had already done the work, and now you will get to gather the harvest."

MANY SAMARITANS BELIEVE

Many Samaritans from the village believed in Jesus because the woman had said, "He told me everything I ever did!" When they came out to see Him, they begged Him to stay in their village. So He stayed for two days, long enough for many more to hear His message and believe. Then they said to the woman, "Now we believe, not just because of what you told us, but because we have heard Him ourselves. Now we know that He is indeed the Savior of the world."

I love so many things about this story. I especially love the way that it reveals the true heart of Jesus, on His way to the next place but intentionally going out of His way to "stumble upon" this Samaritan woman.

We might read this as a normal, everyday occurrence, but it was very unusual for a woman to travel alone to the well and at this time of day. Even in her best attempts to remain unseen and unnoticed, Jesus is present and seeks her out. (Isn't it just like Him to do so!?) Wasting no time, Jesus says to the woman, "Go and get your husband," all the while knowing that speaking to that topic was like pouring salt on a wound. Her shame came quickly, but we can see from the Scriptures that this was the beginning of her freedom. Jesus brought the filthiest, dirtiest, messiest part of her life into the light and then spoke promise to her. What a Father!

Sometimes I think we just need to go to the well, aware that it might be unusual, probably inconvenient, and could ignite our fear. But as we willingly go to Jesus and bring all that we are, we find the deep and unconditional freedom that the living water offers us. Because we know that even as He is calling us out, He is calling us forth, never letting us settle for less than the very best He has to give. Like the Samaritan woman, regardless of our background, our current lifestyle, or the mistakes we have made along the way, freedom is ours to grab hold of. And true freedom? It removes the garment of sadness and the cloak of despair, forcing us to share such wonder with anyone who will listen.

As we willingly go to Jesus and bring all that we are, we find the deep and unconditional freedom that the living water offers us.

PONDER HIS LOVE

1. *Why did Jesus bring up the issue of her multiple husbands? What does this show us about His love?*

2. *What does it mean to "worship in spirit and in truth"?*

3. Jesus says, "The fruit they harvest is people brought to eternal life." Jesus had one mission—to extend His family. What do you consider your harvest? Does it reflect Jesus?

4. For the Samaritan woman, it was her romantic life that brought her shame. Do you have any areas of your life that have proven to be strongholds of shame? What do you think Jesus would tell you if you sat with Him at the well?

5. It was because the woman was willing to be bold and express her newfound freedom to her village that many other Samaritans were saved. Why do you think we are hesitant to speak loudly about our own rescue story?

Dear Lord, wow, I am so grateful for this story of the Samaritan woman and Jesus at the well. I can see myself so much in this story—trying to fulfill obligations and go draw water, making as little sound as possible. *Maybe no one will see me*, I think, but in reality, I am desperately desiring to be seen. Known. The weight of my worry and the shame of my sin overwhelms me at times. I'm sorry for thinking I could hide it from You or that You prefer that. I know You accept all of me at Your feet.

Will You remove me from any place I am hiding and bring light to the surface? Help me engage with truth in the conversations happening inside my own head and with others. Empower me to find a new song to sing over my life and my future.

Thank You for the way You set the captives free. You don't just remove the shackles, Father; You are the wind beneath me giving air to my wings and helping me soar. Strengthen my resolve and set my feet on high places so that I can be a voice of healing for others. I want everything about my life to point to You. Like the Samaritan woman who knew You saw through her soul and loved her the same, help me talk about such love with everyone I know. Is anything greater than advancing Your kingdom?

Today, I celebrate my freedom and the way You lead me to the well so that I may drink and not be thirsty. Only You satisfy my soul.

In the refreshing, kind, and all-knowing name of Jesus, amen.

MEDITATE ON HIS LOVE

GALATIANS 5:1 ESV

For freedom Christ has set us free; stand firm therefore, and do not submit again to a yoke of slavery.

LUKE 4:18–19 ESV

The Spirit of the Lord is upon me, because he has anointed me to proclaim good news to the poor. He has sent me to proclaim liberty to the captives and recovering of sight to the blind, to set at liberty those who are oppressed, to proclaim the year of the Lord's favor.

JOHN 8:31–32 ESV

So Jesus said to the Jews who had believed him, "If you abide in my word, you are truly my disciples, and you will know the truth, and the truth will set you free."

PSALM 34:4–5 ESV

I sought the LORD, and he answered me and delivered me from all my fears. Those who look to him are radiant, and their faces shall never be ashamed.

PSALM 3:3 ESV

But you, O LORD, are a shield about me, my glory, and the lifter of my head.

LEARN ABOUT HIS LOVE

Privileged to Love

JAMES 1:19-2:26 NIV

LISTENING AND DOING

My dear brothers and sisters, take note of this: Everyone should be quick to listen, slow to speak and slow to become angry, because human anger does not produce the righteousness that God desires. Therefore, get rid of all moral filth and the evil that is so prevalent and humbly accept the word planted in you, which can save you.

Do not merely listen to the word, and so deceive yourselves. Do what it says. Anyone who listens to the word but does not do what it says is like someone who looks at his face in a mirror and, after looking at himself, goes away and immediately forgets what he looks like. But whoever looks intently into the perfect law that gives freedom, and continues in it—not forgetting what they have heard, but doing it—they will be blessed in what they do.

Those who consider themselves religious and yet do not keep a tight rein on their tongues deceive themselves, and their religion is worthless. Religion that God our Father accepts as pure and faultless is this: to look after orphans and widows in their distress and to keep oneself from being polluted by the world.

FAVORITISM FORBIDDEN

My brothers and sisters, believers in our glorious Lord Jesus Christ must not show favoritism. Suppose a man comes into your meeting wearing a gold ring and fine clothes, and a poor man in filthy old clothes also comes in. If you show special attention to the man wearing fine clothes and say, "Here's a good seat for you," but say to the poor man, "You stand there" or "Sit on the floor by my feet," have you not discriminated among yourselves and become judges with evil thoughts?

Listen, my dear brothers and sisters: Has not God chosen those who are poor in the eyes of the world to be rich in faith and to inherit the kingdom He promised those who love Him? But you have dishonored the poor. Is it not the rich who are exploiting you? Are they not the ones who are dragging you into court? Are they not the ones who are blaspheming the noble name of Him to whom you belong?

If you really keep the royal law found in Scripture, "Love your neighbor as yourself," you are doing right. But if you show favoritism, you sin and are convicted by the law as lawbreakers. For whoever keeps the whole law and yet stumbles at just one point is guilty of breaking all of it. For he who said, "You shall not commit adultery," also said, "You shall not murder." If you do not commit adultery but do commit murder, you have become a lawbreaker.

Speak and act as those who are going to be judged by the law that gives freedom, because judgment without mercy will be shown to anyone who has not been merciful. Mercy triumphs over judgment.

FAITH AND DEEDS

What good is it, my brothers and sisters, if someone claims to have faith but has no deeds? Can such faith save them? Suppose a brother or a sister is without clothes and daily food. If one of you says to them, "Go in peace; keep warm and well fed," but does nothing about their physical needs, what good is it? In the same way, faith by itself, if it is not accompanied by action, is dead.

But someone will say, "You have faith; I have deeds."

Show me your faith without deeds, and I will show you my faith by my deeds. You believe that there is one God. Good! Even the demons believe that—and shudder.

You foolish person, do you want evidence that faith without deeds is useless? Was not our father Abraham considered righteous for what he did when he offered his son Isaac on the altar? You see that his faith and his actions were working together, and his faith was made complete by what he did. And the Scripture was fulfilled that says, "Abraham believed God, and it was credited to him as righteousness," and he was called God's friend. You see that a person is considered righteous by what they do and not by faith alone.

In the same way, was not even Rahab the prostitute considered righteous for what she did when she gave lodging to the spies and sent them off in a different direction? As the body without the spirit is dead, so faith without deeds is dead.

It's hard to balance, isn't it? Trying to navigate between not performing for God and thinking that we can earn His grace, while also knowing that our faith is not true until we live it out. Because I am a writer and I often write about faith (this you know, obviously), sometimes I get fearful that I will become so accustomed to doing things for God that I will forget that His main priority is spending time with me. The "with" is the game changer here. When James talks about faith in action, he is reminding us that we can't become consumers of truth without letting it transform us. If we do, then we aren't really hearing what it says.

I always notice with my writing that when I anchor myself in His Word and prioritize my time with my Maker, the works of my hands become a reflection of the truth I am pouring into my heart. The discipline is there and the effort is required; however, the stress is removed and the pressure is no longer needed. Love is founded in itself—through loving Jesus, we see that we are loved. It is out of this abiding in Him that we gain the strength, fortitude, discernment, and capability to go and do.

Isn't that so freeing, while also opening the door of great responsibility? We have work to do here. We are to be the helpers and the givers and the people who show up because we know that the Hero of our story has already covered this ground, prepared our inheritance, and whispered to us in response, "Now, go and love just like that."

> When I anchor myself in His Word and prioritize my time with my Maker, the works of my hands become a reflection of the truth that I am pouring into my heart.

PONDER HIS LOVE

1. *Why do you think there is often a disconnect between our faith and our deeds? What reasons do you find to delay deeds?*

2. *How do we become "judges with evil thoughts" of others' clothing and appearance? Have you felt this judgment at times?*

3.   Think about a good deed you have done lately. What set that day apart from others?

4.   James writes that "everyone should be quick to listen, slow to speak and slow to become angry." Which of those three habits would you most like to work on? Ask the Holy Spirit to help you with that one habit.

5.   Scripture says that if we "merely listen to the Word" and yet fail to act, we "deceive ourselves." "Deceive" is such a strong word! How is this verse true?

Dear Lord, thank You for the book of James and the way it reminds me of my authority and responsibility as a child of the King. Your truth is gold and life; my obedience is not an obligation but a privilege.

Will You help me walk in awareness and not deceive my own heart? While correction doesn't always feel good, I know it is Your care and love for me that provide it. Turn my face toward You and align my mind. Break off anything that does not agree with Your Word and Your ways.

My desire to walk in the faith I claim to have is given directly by the Holy Spirit. Thank You for helping me hunger to live in a holy manner. But Father, when I do mess up, will You hold me close? Keep shame far from me but keep repentance close. You have given me the ability to choose something different than what I chose yesterday, and You have crafted my destiny knowing my history. You are not afraid of my mistakes.

Open my eyes to see those around me so that I put the needs of others above myself. Humble my spirit and help me prioritize what You say over everyone else. When my lifestyle conflicts with the hope of heaven, I know You will raise me up and show me a new way.

Thank You for my faith the size of a mustard seed. As I water it, You help it grow. I want to be a giant of faith, a person in whom no storm would make me question my foundation. Will You lead me?

In the effective, vital, and grace-giving name of Jesus, amen.

MEDITATE ON HIS LOVE

MATTHEW 7:13 NLT

You can enter God's Kingdom only through the narrow gate. The highway to hell is broad, and its gate is wide for the many who choose that way.

I PETER 2:15 NLT

It is God's will that your honorable lives should silence those ignorant people who make foolish accusations against you.

PSALM 34:14 NIV

Turn from evil and do good; seek peace and pursue it.

EPHESIANS 6:6 ESV

Not by the way of eye-service, as people-pleasers, but as bondservants of Christ, doing the will of God from the heart.

I CORINTHIANS 15:58 ESV

Therefore, my beloved brothers, be steadfast, immovable, always abounding in the work of the Lord, knowing that in the Lord your labor is not in vain.

LEARN ABOUT HIS LOVE

Redeeming Love

HOSEA 1:2–3:5 NLT

HOSEA'S WIFE AND CHILDREN

When the LORD first began speaking to Israel through Hosea, He said to him, "Go and marry a prostitute, so that some of her children will be conceived in prostitution. This will illustrate how Israel has acted like a prostitute by turning against the LORD and worshiping other gods."

So Hosea married Gomer, the daughter of Diblaim, and she became pregnant and gave Hosea a son. And the LORD said, "Name the child Jezreel, for I am about to punish King Jehu's dynasty to avenge the murders he committed at Jezreel. In fact, I will bring an end to Israel's independence. I will break its military power in the Jezreel Valley."

Soon Gomer became pregnant again and gave birth to a daughter. And the LORD said to Hosea, "Name your daughter Lo-ruhamah—'Not loved'—for I will no longer show love to the people of Israel or forgive them. But I will show love to the people of Judah. I will free them from their enemies—not with weapons and armies or horses and charioteers, but by my power as the LORD their God."

After Gomer had weaned Lo-ruhamah, she again became pregnant and gave birth to a second son. And the LORD said, "Name him Lo-ammi—'Not my people'—for Israel is not my people, and I am not their God.

"Yet the time will come when Israel's people will be like the sands of the seashore—too many to count! Then, at the place where they were told, 'You are not my people,' it will be said, 'You are children of the living God.' Then the people of Judah and Israel will unite together. They will choose one leader for themselves, and they will return from exile together. What a day that will be—the day of Jezreel—when God will again plant His people in His land.

"In that day you will call your brothers Ammi—'My people.' And you will call your sisters Ruhamah—'The ones I love.'"

CHARGES AGAINST AN UNFAITHFUL WIFE

"But now bring charges against Israel—your mother—

> for she is no longer my wife,
> and I am no longer her husband.

Tell her to remove the prostitute's makeup
from her face
    and the clothing that exposes her breasts.

I will punish her for all those times
    when she burned incense to her images of Baal,
when she put on her earrings and jewels
    and went out to look for her lovers
but forgot all about me,"
    says the LORD.

THE LORD'S LOVE FOR UNFAITHFUL ISRAEL

"But then I will win her back once again.
    I will lead her into the desert
    and speak tenderly to her there.
I will return her vineyards to her
    and transform the Valley of Trouble into a
    gateway of hope.
She will give herself to me there,
    as she did long ago when she was young,
    when I freed her from her captivity in Egypt.
When that day comes," says the LORD,
    "you will call me 'my husband'
    instead of 'my master.'
O Israel, I will wipe the many names of Baal from
your lips,
    and you will never mention them again.
On that day I will make a covenant
    with all the wild animals and the birds of the sky
and the animals that scurry along the ground
    so they will not harm you.
I will remove all weapons of war from the land,
    all swords and bows,
so you can live unafraid
    in peace and safety.
I will make you my wife forever,
    showing you righteousness and justice,
    unfailing love and compassion.

I will be faithful to you and make you mine,
    and you will finally know me as the LORD.
In that day, I will answer,"
    says the LORD.
"I will answer the sky as it pleads for clouds.
    And the sky will answer the earth with rain.
Then the earth will answer the thirsty cries
    of the grain, the grapevines, and the olive trees.
And they in turn will answer,
    'Jezreel'—'God plants!'
At that time I will plant a crop of Israelites
    and raise them for myself.
I will show love
    to those I called 'Not loved.'
And to those I called 'Not my people,'
    I will say, 'Now you are my people.'
And they will reply, 'You are our God!'"

HOSEA'S WIFE IS REDEEMED

Then the LORD said to me, "Go and love your wife again, even though she commits adultery with another lover. This will illustrate that the LORD still loves Israel, even though the people have turned to other gods and love to worship them."

So I bought her back for fifteen pieces of silver and five bushels of barley and a measure of wine. Then I said to her, "You must live in my house for many days and stop your prostitution. During this time, you will not have sexual relations with anyone, not even with me."

This shows that Israel will go a long time without a king or prince, and without sacrifices, sacred pillars, priests, or even idols! But afterward the people will return and devote themselves to the LORD their God and to David's descendant, their king. In the last days, they will tremble in awe of the LORD and of His goodness.

I love this love story found in Hosea. It's relatively shocking, as God commands Hosea to marry a prostitute and later take her back into his care, representing the way that Israel committed themselves to God and then turned their backs on Him. The parallels of unfaithfulness between these two scenarios reveal to us the depth of grief and betrayal that God felt about His chosen people. The same way a husband—in this case Hosea—feels about his wife, God feels about His people.

However, it is the lack of faithfulness and integrity that Gomer and Israel displayed that was the invitation to the redemptive power of Jesus. The hard part about redemption is that it is truly one-sided. Israel completely betrayed God, and Gomer was a prostitute that cheated on her husband; what they could give back to those they had betrayed would never have been enough. What I love about God's redeeming love is that it not only forgives us of our mistakes, but it miraculously finds a way to use them. The King of kings never has to remove our history to fulfill our destiny; He takes the broken pieces and makes a new creation.

Redeeming love is just that—it doesn't just forgive what was, it recklessly pursues what can be. It is the majestic ability of the Potter's hands to take fragments and transform them into the brightest and very best future.

> What I love about God's redeeming love is that it not only forgives us of our mistakes, but it miraculously finds a way to use them.

PONDER HIS LOVE

1. What can believers learn from God's call on Hosea's life? How can Hosea's calling encourage us to live as believers?

2. In what ways are you living like Gomer? How might you be turning away from God's love?

3. Redemption requires repentance. How do you repent to God?

4. What do you find most hopeful in this passage? Why?

5. Think about your own story. What is something God has redeemed? What did that journey look like and how does it look now?

Dear Lord, thank You for this story of Hosea and this remarkable reminder of the way Your love redeems even the hardest parts of our hearts and the messiest parts of our lives. Thinking about how You asked Hosea to do something so drastic and so extreme in order that Israel, and now my own heart, can understand the depths of Your love, how do I express gratitude for such a gift?

Will You help me take the time to pause throughout my days and meditate on Your goodness? In every situation and circumstance of my life, You are there. With every mistake I have made, Your forgiveness has covered me. Despite the frailty of my humanity, You don't just forgive my past, You redeem it so that I can fly to new heights. Your grace is scandalous in the way that it touches even the most intimate, difficult, and hard parts of my heart and calls them into the light. I'm so grateful You never give up on me. My value and purpose are solidified in You; great is Your faithfulness.

Help me trust Your forgiveness and Your kindness, not trying to earn my redemption or second-guess whether I deserve it. I am Your child and that is why my feet are secure.

Your love is unconditional, reckless, whole, and true. It is for my life. It is the well that never runs dry, and I am forever welcome there.

In the redeeming, kind, and perfectly loving name of Jesus, amen.

MEDITATE ON HIS LOVE

PSALM 111:9 ESV

He sent redemption to his people; he has commanded his covenant forever. Holy and awesome is his name!

ISAIAH 44:22 ESV

I have blotted out your transgressions like a cloud and your sins like mist; return to me, for I have redeemed you.

JOB 19:25 ESV

For I know that my Redeemer lives, and at the last he will stand upon the earth.

ACTS 20:28 ESV

Pay careful attention to yourselves and to all the flock, in which the Holy Spirit has made you overseers, to care for the church of God, which he obtained with his own blood.

EPHESIANS 1:7 NIV

In Him we have redemption through His blood, the forgiveness of sins, in accordance with the riches of God's grace.

LEARN ABOUT HIS LOVE

Available to Be Assigned

THE BAPTISM AND TEMPTATION OF JESUS

One day Jesus came from Nazareth in Galilee, and John baptized Him in the Jordan River. As Jesus came up out of the water, He saw the heavens splitting apart and the Holy Spirit descending on Him like a dove. And a voice from heaven said, "You are My dearly loved Son, and You bring Me great joy." The Spirit then compelled Jesus to go into the wilderness, where He was tempted by Satan for forty days. He was out among the wild animals, and angels took care of Him.

Later on, after John was arrested, Jesus went into Galilee, where He preached God's Good News. "The time promised by God has come at last!" He announced. "The Kingdom of God is near! Repent of your sins and believe the Good News!"

THE FIRST DISCIPLES

One day as Jesus was walking along the shore of the Sea of Galilee, He saw Simon and His brother Andrew throwing a net into the water, for they fished for a living. Jesus called out to them, "Come, follow me, and I will show you how to fish for people!" And they left their nets at once and followed Him.

A little farther up the shore Jesus saw Zebedee's sons, James and John, in a boat repairing their nets. He called them at once, and they also followed Him, leaving their father, Zebedee, in the boat with the hired men.

JESUS CASTS OUT AN EVIL SPIRIT

Jesus and His companions went to the town of Capernaum. When the Sabbath day came, He went into the synagogue and began to teach. The people were amazed at His teaching, for He taught with real authority—quite unlike the teachers of religious law.

Suddenly, a man in the synagogue who was possessed by an evil spirit cried out, "Why are You interfering with us, Jesus of Nazareth? Have You come to destroy us? I know who You are—the Holy One of God!"

But Jesus reprimanded him. "Be quiet! Come out of the man," He ordered. At that, the evil spirit screamed, threw the man into a convulsion, and then came out of him.

Amazement gripped the audience, and they began to discuss what had happened. "What sort of new teaching is this?" they asked excitedly. "It has such authority! Even evil spirits obey His orders!" The news about Jesus spread quickly throughout the entire region of Galilee.

JESUS HEALS MANY PEOPLE

After Jesus left the synagogue with James and John, they went to Simon and Andrew's home. Now Simon's mother-in-law was sick in bed with a high fever. They told Jesus about her right away. So He went to her bedside, took her by the hand, and helped her sit up. Then the fever left her, and she prepared a meal for them.

That evening after sunset, many sick and demon-possessed people were brought to Jesus. The whole town gathered at the door to watch. So Jesus healed many people who were sick with various diseases, and He cast out many demons. But because the demons knew who He was, He did not allow them to speak.

JESUS PREACHES IN GALILEE

Before daybreak the next morning, Jesus got up and went out to an isolated place to pray. Later Simon and the others went out to find Him. When they found Him, they said, "Everyone is looking for you."

But Jesus replied, "We must go on to other towns as well, and I will preach to them, too. That is why I came." So He traveled throughout the region of Galilee, preaching in the synagogues and casting out demons.

JESUS HEALS A MAN WITH LEPROSY

A man with leprosy came and knelt in front of Jesus, begging to be healed. "If You are willing, You can heal me and make me clean," he said.

Moved with compassion, Jesus reached out and touched him. "I am willing," He said. "Be healed!" Instantly the leprosy disappeared, and the man was healed. Then Jesus sent him on his way with a stern warning: "Don't tell anyone about this. Instead, go to the priest and let him examine you. Take along the offering required in the law of Moses for those who have been healed of leprosy. This will be a public testimony that you have been cleansed."

But the man went and spread the word, proclaiming to everyone what had happened. As a result, large crowds soon surrounded Jesus, and He couldn't publicly enter a town anywhere. He had to stay out in the secluded places, but people from everywhere kept coming to Him.

It's hard to believe that such significant and life-changing events happened for so many people within just one chapter of the Bible. One miracle after another occurs as Jesus and His disciples walk through the village streets and go from home to home. It's easy to get caught up in the awe of the miracles, which is warranted; however, what strikes me as profoundly gracious is the availability of the Miracle-worker.

When I think about my own life and reflect on my past, there is a common thread running through all the times when God used me to help others: I was available. Though I had my own plans and desires, it is obvious when I made myself available to be used by Jesus, wherever and whenever He desired.

A more recent example actually came to mind when I was reading this story. I was planning a wedding, powering through some big deadlines for work, and dealing with several family happenings. However, I had a friend walking through a really tough time, and I knew the Lord was prompting my heart. "Hey Cleere, you're in ministry, right? This is it. I'll help you recoup your time."

I decided to show up every morning and pray with her for a week, thinking maybe that would help her heart feel loved. Little did I know, God was working a miracle inside of me. As I realized how often I base my availability on my convenience and preference, God helped me see that Jesus' miracles are always possible because He is available. What a gift to us, that Jesus, the greatest Helper of all, is always by our side.

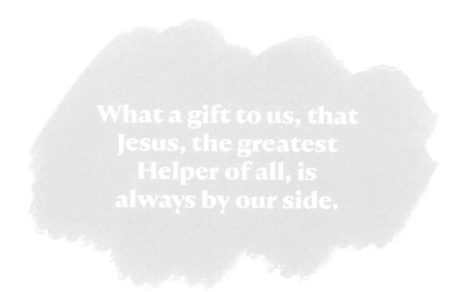

What a gift to us, that Jesus, the greatest Helper of all, is always by our side.

1. *This Scripture passage begins with Jesus being baptized by the Holy Spirit and God saying, "You are my dearly loved Son, and You bring Me great joy." How do you find comfort in knowing God was proud of Jesus before He ever performed one miracle on earth?*

2. *Andrew and Simon were brothers and fishermen; obviously they had lived this lifestyle for a while. But when Jesus came by, they immediately followed Him. What does this show about Jesus and His Spirit? What does this reveal about Andrew's and Simon's availability?*

3. *Jesus spoke with authority, which captivated the village people. What do you think that means?*

4. *What does it mean to be "available" in your current lifestyle? What might distract you from that?*

5. *When the man with leprosy reached out to be healed, Jesus said, "I am willing." Does this mean He had to be in agreement before it could happen? Was there a transfer of power? What do you think?*

Dear Lord, thank You for Your Word and every sentence included in Scripture. I am overwhelmed at the way it guides me and comforts me exactly where I am and wherever I find myself. Reading the Gospel of Mark, I am amazed at how normal these miracles were for Jesus. As He went from place to place, He worked life-altering miracles that changed the trajectory of every person involved and the eternity of all who believed. Sometimes, it is hard to imagine such miracles in my present-day life, but I want to believe for them. Will You help me?

I'm reminded that Jesus' secret weapon was His availability. His healing power was seen because He was aware; He was aware because His Spirit was available to be used and led by You, Father. I want to live like this. I fear sometimes that if I stop, I won't have enough time to get to the next destination. But You, Lord? You hold time in Your hands.

Broaden my view so that I can see the world and Your people. Solidify my steps so that I stay on the path You have for me, not veering to the right nor the left. I don't have to fear being disqualified; where You position me, You equip me to serve. Help me trust that.

Thank You for the blessing of an able body, a sound mind, a peaceful soul, a caring heart, and willing feet. Where You lead, I'll follow. Available to You—that is my mission.

In the mighty, gracious, and available name of Jesus, amen.

MEDITATE ON HIS LOVE

ISAIAH 6:8 ESV

I heard the voice of the Lord saying, "Whom shall I send, and who will go for us?" Then I said, "Here am I! Send me."

ROMANS 12:1 ESV

I appeal to you therefore, brothers, by the mercies of God, to present your bodies as a living sacrifice, holy and acceptable to God, which is your spiritual worship.

II TIMOTHY 4:2 ESV

Preach the word; be ready in season and out of season; reprove, rebuke, and exhort, with complete patience and teaching.

MATTHEW 9:9 ESV

As Jesus passed on from there, he saw a man called Matthew sitting at the tax booth, and he said to him, "Follow me." And he rose and followed him.

II CORINTHIANS 9:7 ESV

Each one must give as he has decided in his heart, not reluctantly or under compulsion, for God loves a cheerful giver.

LEARN ABOUT HIS LOVE

Transformed by Love

ROMANS 12:1—13:14 NIV

Therefore, I urge you, brothers and sisters, in view of God's mercy, to offer your bodies as a living sacrifice, holy and pleasing to God—this is your true and proper worship. Do not conform to the pattern of this world, but be transformed by the renewing of your mind. Then you will be able to test and approve what God's will is—His good, pleasing and perfect will.

HUMBLE SERVICE IN THE BODY OF CHRIST

For by the grace given me I say to every one of you: Do not think of yourself more highly than you ought, but rather think of yourself with sober judgment, in accordance with the faith God has distributed to each of you. For just as each of us has one body with many members, and these members do not all have the same function, so in Christ we, though many, form one body, and each member belongs to all the others. We have different gifts, according to the grace given to each of us. If your gift is prophesying, then prophesy in accordance with your faith; if it is serving, then serve; if it is teaching, then teach; if it is to encourage, then give encouragement; if it is giving, then give generously; if it is to lead, do it diligently; if it is to show mercy, do it cheerfully.

LOVE IN ACTION

Love must be sincere. Hate what is evil; cling to what is good. Be devoted to one another in love. Honor one another above yourselves. Never be lacking in zeal, but keep your spiritual fervor, serving the Lord. Be joyful in hope, patient in affliction, faithful in prayer. Share with the Lord's people who are in need. Practice hospitality.

Bless those who persecute you; bless and do not curse. Rejoice with those who rejoice; mourn with those who mourn. Live in harmony with one another. Do not be proud, but be willing to associate with people of low position. Do not be conceited.

Do not repay anyone evil for evil. Be careful to do what is right in the eyes of everyone. If it is possible, as far as it depends on you, live at peace with everyone. Do not take revenge, my dear friends, but leave room for God's wrath, for it is written: "It is Mine to avenge; I will repay," says the Lord. On the contrary:

"If your enemy is hungry, feed him;
if he is thirsty, give him something to drink.
In doing this, you will heap burning coals on
his head."

Do not be overcome by evil, but overcome evil
with good.

Let everyone be subject to the governing
authorities, for there is no authority except that
which God has established. The authorities that
exist have been established by God. Consequently,
whoever rebels against the authority is rebelling
against what God has instituted, and those who
do so will bring judgment on themselves. For
rulers hold no terror for those who do right, but
for those who do wrong. Do you want to be free
from fear of the one in authority? Then do what
is right and you will be commended. For the one
in authority is God's servant for your good. But
if you do wrong, be afraid, for rulers do not bear
the sword for no reason. They are God's servants,
agents of wrath to bring punishment on the
wrongdoer. Therefore, it is necessary to submit
to the authorities, not only because of possible
punishment but also as a matter of conscience.

This is also why you pay taxes, for the authorities
are God's servants, who give their full time
to governing. Give to everyone what you owe
them: If you owe taxes, pay taxes; if revenue,
then revenue; if respect, then respect; if honor,
then honor.

LOVE FULFILLS THE LAW

Let no debt remain outstanding, except the con-
tinuing debt to love one another, for whoever
loves others has fulfilled the law. The command-
ments, "You shall not commit adultery," "You
shall not murder," "You shall not steal," "You shall
not covet," and whatever other command there
may be, are summed up in this one command:
"Love your neighbor as yourself." Love does no
harm to a neighbor. Therefore love is the fulfill-
ment of the law.

THE DAY IS NEAR

And do this, understanding the present time: The
hour has already come for you to wake up from
your slumber, because our salvation is nearer now
than when we first believed. The night is nearly
over; the day is almost here. So let us put aside
the deeds of darkness and put on the armor of
light. Let us behave decently, as in the daytime,
not in carousing and drunkenness, not in sexual
immorality and debauchery, not in dissension
and jealousy. Rather, clothe yourselves with the
Lord Jesus Christ, and do not think about how to
gratify the desires of the flesh.

When we think about our own qualities and establishing better habits for our lives, we tend to think about them through the lens of the word "change." By means of behavior modification, we will do better, right? Change tends to go after behavior, while transformation seeks to redefine what we value. I think that's the hard part about our flesh and the gospel: We so desperately want to change for Jesus, because it's easy and appealing to alter what is on the surface. But our Maker? He calls for a total overhaul of the heart, a transformation from the inside out.

I know that the human kind of love that I can offer may temporarily satisfy another, but when I can love others from the overflow of love I have received from Jesus? That is different. That is the kind of love that transforms relationships, sees people for their potential, and steps out in faith regardless of what is reciprocated.

When I think about my life, the areas where I am still struggling to experience full transformation are the ones where I am clinging more tightly to my human effort of behavior modification than I am surrendering to the power of Jesus. I have failed to do better, but I am desperate to prove that I can stay on the tightrope rather than fall into Jesus. Can you relate to this?

Our doing comes from our believing. God's desire, made obvious by these Scriptures, is to transform the believing so the doing follows. Reminding my own heart of this, I am challenged to stop the reputation management—of myself and others—and ask, "Hey God, can You refresh me in this area?"

> The human kind of love that I can offer may temporarily satisfy another, but when I can love others from the overflow of love I have received from Jesus? That is different.

PONDER HIS LOVE

1. *Have you ever thought about "put[ting] on the armor of light" when you dress for the day ahead? What would that mean for you?*

2. *Is there a particular area that comes to mind when you think about the transforming power of Jesus? Maybe a struggle you've accepted as a "thorn" that Jesus wants to work through? What is it? Are you willing to surrender it?*

3. *"Be devoted to one another in love" requires joyful attention and eagerness to love. How does devotion reflect the heart of Jesus?*

4. *The Scripture reading points out that we are to pay others what we owe them, whether that be money, honor, or respect. How could following that guidance leave you more refreshed?*

5. *What does it mean to be "transformed by the renewing of your mind"? How do you think that happens?*

Dear Lord, thank You for this calling out and calling forth of what You desire for my life. I want to follow You instead of what the world prompts me to do and say. Why is it that I do what my flesh tells me, despite knowing Your way is life? Help me. Thank You for forgiving me every time I forget but also for continually reminding me of my righteousness in You. Your sacrifice doesn't give me a free pass to do what I like; it is the freedom to choose what is good over what is easy, what is holy over what is popular, and what is life-giving over what is pleasurable.

When I rise in the morning, first thing—will You humble my spirit? Remind me that I need You and renew my thoughts from yesterday. Help me seek You so that my time will be filled with learning Your character instead of trying to change my circumstances. Because I know that as I learn who You are, You will show me who I am and what to do.

Transforming my perspective, You show me how to see others. Thank You for this gift. Give me the supernatural knack to empathize and see their heart as You do, Father. Steer me in the way of people's needs so that I can be a steward of my resources and someone who points to Your divine provision.

Release my striving to be perfect and re-engage my zeal, knowing that Your perfection covers my gaps.

Help me live an honorable life, working hard and staying focused on You, because in doing so, others will know the transformation You've made in me.

In the life-changing, life-giving, and life-restoring name of Jesus, amen.

MEDITATE ON HIS LOVE

PROVERBS 15:33 NIV

Wisdom's instruction is to fear the LORD, and humility comes before honor.

I CORINTHIANS 8:1 NIV

We know that "We all possess knowledge." But knowledge puffs up while love builds up.

EZEKIEL 36:26 ESV

I will give you a new heart, and a new spirit I will put within you. And I will remove the heart of stone from your flesh and give you a heart of flesh.

ISAIAH 26:3 NIV

You will keep in perfect peace those whose minds are steadfast, because they trust in You.

PSALM 139:23–24 ESV

Search me, O God, and know my heart! Try me and know my thoughts! And see if there be any grievous way in me, and lead me in the way everlasting!

LEARN ABOUT HIS LOVE

Intimacy Brings Belief

1 KINGS 17:1–24; 18:41–46 NLT

ELIJAH FED BY RAVENS

Now Elijah, who was from Tishbe in Gilead, told King Ahab, "As surely as the LORD, the God of Israel, lives—the God I serve—there will be no dew or rain during the next few years until I give the word!"

Then the LORD said to Elijah, "Go to the east and hide by Kerith Brook, near where it enters the Jordan River. Drink from the brook and eat what the ravens bring you, for I have commanded them to bring you food."

So Elijah did as the LORD told him and camped beside Kerith Brook, east of the Jordan. The ravens brought him bread and meat each morning and evening, and he drank from the brook. But after a while the brook dried up, for there was no rainfall anywhere in the land.

THE WIDOW AT ZAREPHATH

Then the LORD said to Elijah, "Go and live in the village of Zarephath, near the city of Sidon. I have instructed a widow there to feed you."

So he went to Zarephath. As he arrived at the gates of the village, he saw a widow gathering sticks, and he asked her, "Would you please bring me a little water in a cup?" As she was going to get it, he called to her, "Bring me a bite of bread, too."

But she said, "I swear by the LORD your God that I don't have a single piece of bread in the house. And I have only a handful of flour left in the jar and a little cooking oil in the bottom of the jug. I was just gathering a few sticks to cook this last meal, and then my son and I will die."

But Elijah said to her, "Don't be afraid! Go ahead and do just what you've said, but make a little bread for me first. Then use what's left to prepare a meal for yourself and your son. For this is what the LORD, the God of Israel, says: There will always be flour and olive oil left in your containers until the time when the LORD sends rain and the crops grow again!"

So she did as Elijah said, and she and Elijah and her family continued to eat for many days. There was always enough flour and olive oil left in the containers, just as the LORD had promised through Elijah.

Some time later the woman's son became sick. He grew worse and worse, and finally he died. Then she said to Elijah, "O man of God, what have you done to me? Have you come here to point out my sins and kill my son?"

But Elijah replied, "Give me your son." And he took the child's body from her arms, carried him up the stairs to the room where he was staying, and laid the body on his bed. Then Elijah cried out to the LORD, "O LORD my God, why have You brought tragedy to this widow who has opened her home to me, causing her son to die?"

And he stretched himself out over the child three times and cried out to the LORD, "O LORD my God, please let this child's life return to him." The LORD heard Elijah's prayer, and the life of the child returned, and he revived! Then Elijah brought him down from the upper room and gave him to his mother. "Look!" he said. "Your son is alive!"

Then the woman told Elijah, "Now I know for sure that you are a man of God, and that the LORD truly speaks through you.". . .

ELIJAH PRAYS FOR RAIN

Then Elijah said to Ahab, "Go get something to eat and drink, for I hear a mighty rainstorm coming!"

So Ahab went to eat and drink. But Elijah climbed to the top of Mount Carmel and bowed low to the ground and prayed with his face between his knees.

Then he said to his servant, "Go and look out toward the sea."

The servant went and looked, then returned to Elijah and said, "I didn't see anything."

Seven times Elijah told him to go and look. Finally the seventh time, his servant told him, "I saw a little cloud about the size of a man's hand rising from the sea."

Then Elijah shouted, "Hurry to Ahab and tell him, 'Climb into your chariot and go back home. If you don't hurry, the rain will stop you!'"

And soon the sky was black with clouds. A heavy wind brought a terrific rainstorm, and Ahab left quickly for Jezreel. Then the LORD gave special strength to Elijah. He tucked his cloak into his belt and ran ahead of Ahab's chariot all the way to the entrance of Jezreel.

There are so many things that stand out about Elijah and his life in the Bible. It's incredible. The back story on Elijah is that he was ordinary, like you and me, and he was a prophet. Reading the miracles that happen in Elijah's life, we can easily brush over them as though they are expected. However, to do so is shortcutting the strong faith that Elijah had in the Lord. It is obvious that Elijah and the Lord had an intimate relationship, as Elijah heard God guiding him with each and every step. Not only did Elijah trust His heavenly Father in the good times, he willingly set out into the wilderness and believed for God's provision in the lean times.

We see that Elijah's faith not only anchored his life but provided the setup for a miracle for the widow's son. How could Elijah have managed to perform such a miracle? Because of his closeness to the heart of the Father. God heard his prayer and preserved the boy's life. Later, we see that Elijah prays for rain and when the tiniest cloud appears, he believes God has heard his prayer. When the rainstorm comes, God gives Elijah special strength and fortitude to make it to his destination.

I love Elijah, don't you? His story prompts me to ask myself, "When God calls you to do the unconventional, do you question whether it's Him?" Elijah believed three things: that God loved Him, that God was all-powerful, and that God was trustworthy. The combination provided Elijah with the perfect setup to refresh the hearts of those he came across as he ran hand-in-hand with his God.

Elijah's faith not only anchored his life but provided the setup for a miracle for the widow's son.

1.   *God sent Elijah to the wilderness first. Why do you think He did this? What do you think it proved to Elijah about God?*

2.   *Scripture says that the ravens brought food to Elijah each morning, forcing daily dependence upon God's provision. Would this be hard for you? Do you find yourself fearing scarcity?*

3. *Elijah does what he believes God tells him to do. His intimacy with God helps him hear His voice. How does your current lifestyle support you leaning in and listening to Him?*

4. *Before Elijah revived the boy, he lay over him three times and cried out to God. He was never afraid to express his sentiments and his dependence on God. Do you believe God still works miracles? Do you think He works them through you?*

5. *Elijah had prayed to God and believed the rain was coming, forcing his servant to look again seven times. How do you see Elijah's unwavering belief impacting the lives of others like the servant, the widow, and the widow's son?*

Dear Lord, thank You for Your servant Elijah and his story shared throughout the pages of Scripture. It challenges and comforts my soul to think that he was just like me and he bravely followed Your call, whatever that meant for his life.

You always gave him direction, Father. I know You do the same for me; it's just sometimes I wonder if I am hearing You correctly or if I am fearing what will happen when I get to the other side. Will You help me in my unbelief? Lead me back to the truth of Your character and the purity of Your heart. I know You will never abandon me.

Help me cultivate the kind of intimacy that asks my friends to "Go look again!" because I know that You will show up, just as You promised. Thank You for inviting me to sit with You, learn from You, and be with You. In receiving Your love, I find the confidence to live a life of love, marveling at the fact that the King of kings is directing me. The One who knit me in my mother's womb, knows the number of hairs on my head, and loves me more than the sand on the seashore—that is the Commander of heaven's armies and He is with me!

Like Elijah's, make my life an example to those around me. You are my miracle worker, my Maker, and my Master. My life is Yours; great is Your faithfulness.

In the miraculous, hopeful, and intimate name of Jesus, amen.

MEDITATE ON HIS LOVE

JOHN 17:22–23 ESV

The glory that you have given me I have given to them, that they may be one even as we are one, I in them and you in me, that they may become perfectly one, so that the world may know that you sent me and loved them even as you loved me.

JEREMIAH 31:3 ESV

The LORD appeared to him from far away. I have loved you with an everlasting love; therefore I have continued my faithfulness to you.

REVELATION 3:20 ESV

Behold, I stand at the door and knock. If anyone hears my voice and opens the door, I will come in to him and eat with him, and he with me.

PHILIPPIANS 3:7–8 ESV

But whatever gain I had, I counted as loss for the sake of Christ. Indeed, I count everything as loss because of the surpassing worth of knowing Christ Jesus my Lord. For his sake I have suffered the loss of all things and count them as rubbish, in order that I may gain Christ.

For more on this topic, scan the QR code for a video message from Cleere.

LEARN ABOUT HIS LOVE

Dependence Invites Abundance

EXODUS 16:1-31 NLT

MANNA AND QUAIL FROM HEAVEN

Then the whole community of Israel set out from Elim and journeyed into the wilderness of Sin, between Elim and Mount Sinai. They arrived there on the fifteenth day of the second month, one month after leaving the land of Egypt. There, too, the whole community of Israel complained about Moses and Aaron.

"If only the LORD *had killed us back in Egypt," they moaned. "There we sat around pots filled with meat and ate all the bread we wanted. But now you have brought us into this wilderness to starve us all to death."*

Then the LORD *said to Moses, "Look, I'm going to rain down food from heaven for you. Each day the people can go out and pick up as much food as they need for that day. I will test them in this to see whether or not they will follow My instructions. On the sixth day they will gather food, and when they prepare it, there will be twice as much as usual."*

So Moses and Aaron said to all the people of Israel, "By evening you will realize it was the LORD *who brought you out of the land of Egypt. In the morning you will see the*

glory of the LORD, *because He has heard your complaints, which are against Him, not against us. What have we done that you should complain about us?" Then Moses added, "The* LORD *will give you meat to eat in the evening and bread to satisfy you in the morning, for He has heard all your complaints against Him. What have we done? Yes, your complaints are against the* LORD, *not against us."*

Then Moses said to Aaron, "Announce this to the entire community of Israel: 'Present yourselves before the LORD, *for He has heard your complaining.'" And as Aaron spoke to the whole community of Israel, they looked out toward the wilderness. There they could see the awesome glory of the* LORD *in the cloud.*

Then the LORD *said to Moses, "I have heard the Israelites' complaints. Now tell them, 'In the evening you will have meat to eat, and in the morning you will have all the bread you want. Then you will know that I am the* LORD *your God.'"*

That evening vast numbers of quail flew in and covered the camp. And the next morning the area around the camp was wet with dew. When the dew evaporated, a flaky substance as fine as frost blanketed the ground. The Israelites were puzzled when they saw it. "What is it?" they asked each other. They had no idea what it was.

And Moses told them, "It is the food the Lord has given you to eat. These are the Lord's instructions: Each household should gather as much as it needs. Pick up two quarts for each person in your tent."

So the people of Israel did as they were told. Some gathered a lot, some only a little. But when they measured it out, everyone had just enough. Those who gathered a lot had nothing left over, and those who gathered only a little had enough. Each family had just what it needed.

Then Moses told them, "Do not keep any of it until morning." But some of them didn't listen and kept some of it until morning. But by then it was full of maggots and had a terrible smell. Moses was very angry with them.

After this the people gathered the food morning by morning, each family according to its need. And as the sun became hot, the flakes they had not picked up melted and disappeared. On the sixth day, they gathered twice as much as usual—four quarts for each person instead of two. Then all the leaders of the community came and asked Moses for an explanation. He told them, "This is what the Lord commanded: Tomorrow will

be a day of complete rest, a holy Sabbath day set apart for the Lord. So bake or boil as much as you want today, and set aside what is left for tomorrow."

So they put some aside until morning, just as Moses had commanded. And in the morning the leftover food was wholesome and good, without maggots or odor. Moses said, "Eat this food today, for today is a Sabbath day dedicated to the Lord. There will be no food on the ground today. You may gather the food for six days, but the seventh day is the Sabbath. There will be no food on the ground that day."

Some of the people went out anyway on the seventh day, but they found no food. The Lord asked Moses, "How long will these people refuse to obey My commands and instructions? They must realize that the Sabbath is the Lord's gift to you. That is why He gives you a two-day supply on the sixth day, so there will be enough for two days. On the Sabbath day you must each stay in your place. Do not go out to pick up food on the seventh day." So the people did not gather any food on the seventh day.

The Israelites called the food manna. It was white like coriander seed, and it tasted like honey wafers.

This story begins after Moses led the people of Israel through the Red Sea. Literally the sea parted and they crossed through on dry ground. Then they arrive at this new place and everyone is complaining about Moses and Aaron and their leadership, as they now have little food and water. However, we see that Moses and Aaron were perfectly aware of these conditions, knowing that if God had led them to this place, He would provide for His people.

The Lord sent bread and meat in the form of quail and manna and instructed everyone to gather what they needed for each day and nothing more. We see that every family had exactly what they needed, and those who tried to store up for the next day found their food infested and destroyed by morning. It's obvious that God was trying to help the stubborn and forgetful people of Israel see that He would not abandon them, even in the wilderness. Because He is God, He knows that our flesh often requires force in order to practice dependence.

Reading this, I find myself wondering, *Would I be one of those trying to store up food out of fear that God might not show up tomorrow?* I would like to think that I would trust His faithfulness, especially after days and days of provision. Just as God supplied for their needs in an unconventional way they weren't expecting, He often shows up in unpredictable and unprecedented ways to remind us that He is God and we are not.

I have seen that when I depend on Him and His supply, He always gives in abundance. Each day, I have all that I need; not because I am faithful but because His love never changes. Walking in the confidence and courage that Jesus will show up for us, we are able to become love in action to the world around us.

Each day, I have all that I need; not because I am faithful but because His love never changes.

1. *As mentioned, God had just brought the people through the Red Sea and performed a miracle. Why do you think they were so quick to forget? What does this show us about the nature of sin?*

2. *The people of God direct their frustration at Moses and Aaron, but really they are frustrated at God. How can you relate to this through the lens of Moses and Aaron as leaders or the people as followers?*

3. What rules were the people given for collecting the manna? What was the point of these rules? What do you think God was trying to teach them?

4. The manna was provided by God but the people still had to gather it. What principle does this reveal to you?

5. In what area of your life do you struggle the most to depend on God? Why is that? How can you practice surrender?

Dear Lord, thank You for this story about Moses, Aaron, and the people of Israel. I love how You make everything in Your Word relatable and helpful, even when I don't realize it at the time.

Reading about the people of Israel, I am reminded of myself. How quick am I to forget Your miracles and the provision You have given at every moment in my life! Will You forgive me? Help me surrender my fear and bitterness so that I can see and witness Your goodness in the land of the living. Remind me to reflect on Your kindness so that I never forget how many times You have saved me. Help me have an attitude of gratitude and keep a song of praise on my lips.

Thank You for this reminder of daily dependence and the richness that it brings. You always provide what I need; Your supply does not run dry and Your awareness of my needs is ever present. Activate my faith and help me expect Your faithfulness. I love that You provide for me in unconventional and unpredictable ways, reminding me that You are God and I am not. Remove my desire to white-knuckle my way to the other side because I know that Your way is best.

Depending on You, I come to know what life truly means. Your arms are mighty and tender and nothing is too hard for You, Father. How blessed am I to be a child of the King.

In the dependable, faithful, and all-knowing name of Jesus, amen.

MEDITATE ON HIS LOVE

PROVERBS 16:9 NIV

In their hearts humans plan their course, but the LORD establishes their steps.

MATTHEW 6:34 NIV

Therefore do not worry about tomorrow, for tomorrow will worry about itself. Each day has enough trouble of its own.

HEBREWS 4:16 ESV

Let us then with confidence draw near to the throne of grace, that we may receive mercy and find grace to help in time of need.

PSALM 80:19 NIV

Restore us, LORD God Almighty; make your face shine on us, that we may be saved.

LAMENTATIONS 3:22–26 ESV

The steadfast love of the LORD never ceases; his mercies never come to an end; they are new every morning; great is your faithfulness. "The LORD is my portion," says my soul, "therefore I will hope in him." The LORD is good to those who wait for him, to the soul who seeks him. It is good that one should wait quietly for the salvation of the LORD.

LEARN ABOUT HIS LOVE

Fragility Invites Strength

For what we preach is not ourselves, but Jesus Christ as Lord, and ourselves as your servants for Jesus' sake. For God, who said, "Let light shine out of darkness," made His light shine in our hearts to give us the light of the knowledge of God's glory displayed in the face of Christ.

But we have this treasure in jars of clay to show that this all-surpassing power is from God and not from us. We are hard pressed on every side, but not crushed; perplexed, but not in despair; persecuted, but not abandoned; struck down, but not destroyed. We always carry around in our body the death of Jesus, so that the life of Jesus may also be revealed in our body. For we who are alive are always being given over to death for Jesus' sake, so that His life may also be revealed in our mortal body. So then, death is at work in us, but life is at work in you.

It is written: "I believed; therefore I have spoken." Since we have that same spirit of faith, we also believe and therefore speak, because we know that the One who raised the Lord Jesus from the dead will also raise us with Jesus and present us with you to Himself. All this is for your benefit, so that the grace that is reaching more and more people may cause thanksgiving to overflow to the glory of God.

Therefore we do not lose heart. Though outwardly we are wasting away, yet inwardly we are being renewed day by day. For our light and momentary troubles are achieving for us an eternal glory that far outweighs them all. So we fix our eyes not on what is seen, but on what is unseen, since what is seen is temporary, but what is unseen is eternal . . . .

AWAITING THE NEW BODY

For we know that if the earthly tent we live in is destroyed, we have a building from God, an eternal house in heaven, not built by human hands. Meanwhile we groan, longing to be clothed instead with our heavenly dwelling, because when we are clothed, we will not be found naked. For while we are in this tent, we groan and are burdened, because we do not wish to be unclothed but to be clothed instead with our heavenly dwelling, so that what is mortal may be swallowed up by life. Now the One who has fashioned us for this very purpose is God, who has given us the Spirit as a deposit, guaranteeing what is to come.

Therefore we are always confident and know that as long as we are at home in the body we are away from the Lord. For we live by faith, not by sight. We are confident, I say, and would prefer to be away from the body and at home with the Lord. So we make it our goal to please Him, whether we are at home in the body or away from it. For we must all appear before the judgment seat of Christ, so that each of us may receive what is due us for the things done while in the body, whether good or bad . . .

As God's co-workers we urge you not to receive God's grace in vain. For He says,

"In the time of My favor I heard you,
and in the day of salvation I helped you."

I tell you, now is the time of God's favor, now is the day of salvation.

PAUL'S HARDSHIPS

We put no stumbling block in anyone's path, so that our ministry will not be discredited. Rather, as servants of God we commend ourselves in every way: in great endurance; in troubles, hardships and distresses; in beatings, imprisonments and riots; in hard work, sleepless nights and hunger; in purity, understanding, patience and kindness; in the Holy Spirit and in sincere love; in truthful speech and in the power of God; with weapons of righteousness in the right hand and in the left; through glory and dishonor, bad report and good report; genuine, yet regarded as impostors; known, yet regarded as unknown; dying, and yet we live on; beaten, and yet not killed; sorrowful, yet always rejoicing; poor, yet making many rich; having nothing, and yet possessing everything.

Sometimes I get frustrated by my own fragility. I feel the weight of my own weakness and it feels overwhelming, especially when I'm struggling. Sometimes I think back on my prayers and realize that I wasn't praying for God to intervene; rather, I was praying that God would make me strong enough so I didn't need Him. It is the notion of praying to a perfect God for the same perfection only He has, when it was He who created imperfect people so that they would be required to seek Him. Isn't that ironic?

However, the more I read Scripture and dig into the stories of the people God used all throughout the pages of His Word, I am reminded that it is actually my weaknesses that invite His strength because the only way to become empowered is to be in need of power. As I discover, with each day that passes, how temporary my earthly vessel and home is, I learn to redirect my energy toward building God's kingdom.

The struggles will come—they are promised! The pressure will rise—that is guaranteed! However, because He lives in me, I get to tap into His strength, use His supply, and work with Him to do great things. I find so much joy and freedom in knowing that no matter how loud my insecurity yells or how severe my brokenness feels, God can still use a wretch like me. The Father's love knows no bounds, and His grace? It really can cover everything that I lack. What a comfort that is!

> Because He lives in me,
> I get to tap into His strength,
> use His supply, and work
> with Him to do great things.

1. *Scripture tells us that we are jars of clay. Why do you think the writers used that analogy?*

2. *This passage mentions that our outward selves are wasting away. Culture puts a high value on our outward appearance, reputation, and status. Do you find it hard to keep up? Why or why not?*

3. It says that we ache to be clothed with our heavenly dwelling. What do you think that means?

4. What does it mean to be God's coworker? Have you thought about your relationship with Him in that way?

5. What tends to overwhelm you the most? How can you seek Jesus' power in that place?

Dear Lord, thank You for this incredible and timely reminder of my own brokenness and need for You. Even though I know that You made me, sometimes I feel like I might surprise You by my weakness, or You might change your mind about using me or claiming me. I find that my flesh desires perfection more than I realize, and it leaves me discouraged, insecure, and afraid.

But You, Father, You lead me back to truth. You remind me that while my body may be wasting away and the things around me are temporary, my spirit is being renewed by Your truth and heaven is gaining ground.

Will You help me be bold and proactive where I am, even when I feel ill-equipped? Show me what to put my hands, heart, and mind to so that I may please You.

Grant me the supernatural vision to see You, even in the driest and dullest of places. Cultivate in me a warrior spirit that perseveres and persists because it knows You are fighting for me.

Thank You for assuring my mind when I am overwhelmed. Thank You for caring for my heart when I am fearful. Thank You for empowering me with the strength of heaven behind me, the angels guarding me, and the Holy Spirit living and active inside of me.

Great are You, Lord. When I am weak, You are strong.

In the empowering, humble, and loving name of Jesus, Amen.

MEDITATE ON HIS LOVE

EZEKIEL 36:27 NASB

I will put My Spirit within you and cause you to walk in My statutes, and you will be careful to observe My ordinances.

I TIMOTHY 1:12 NASB

I thank Christ Jesus our Lord, who has strengthened me, because He considered me faithful, putting me into service.

II TIMOTHY 4:17 NASB

But the Lord stood with me and strengthened me, so that through me the proclamation might be fully accomplished, and that all the Gentiles might hear; and I was rescued out of the lion's mouth.

I PETER 5:10 NASB

After you have suffered for a little while, the God of all grace, who called you to His eternal glory in Christ, will Himself perfect, confirm, strengthen and establish you.

ISAIAH 40:28–31 ESV

Have you not known? Have you not heard? The LORD is the everlasting God, the Creator of the ends of the earth. He does not faint or grow weary; his understanding is unsearchable. He gives power to the faint, and to him who has no might he increases strength. Even youths shall faint and be weary, and young men shall fall exhausted; but they who wait for the LORD shall renew their strength; they shall mount up with wings like eagles; they shall run and not be weary; they shall walk and not faint.

LEARN ABOUT HIS LOVE

Teamwork Makes the Dream Work

ACTS 18:1–28; ROMANS 16:1–5;
1 CORINTHIANS 16:19 NIV

After this, Paul left Athens and went to Corinth. There he met a Jew named Aquila, a native of Pontus, who had recently come from Italy with his wife Priscilla, because Claudius had ordered all Jews to leave Rome. Paul went to see them, and because he was a tentmaker as they were, he stayed and worked with them. Every Sabbath he reasoned in the synagogue, trying to persuade Jews and Greeks.

When Silas and Timothy came from Macedonia, Paul devoted himself exclusively to preaching, testifying to the Jews that Jesus was the Messiah. But when they opposed Paul and became abusive, he shook out his clothes in protest and said to them, "Your blood be on your own heads! I am innocent of it. From now on I will go to the Gentiles."

Then Paul left the synagogue and went next door to the house of Titius Justus, a worshiper of God. Crispus, the synagogue leader, and his entire household believed in the Lord; and many of the Corinthians who heard Paul believed and were baptized.

One night the Lord spoke to Paul in a vision: "Do not be afraid; keep on speaking, do not be silent. For I am with you, and no one is going to attack and harm you, because I have many people in this city." So Paul stayed in Corinth for a year and a half, teaching them the word of God.

While Gallio was proconsul of Achaia, the Jews of Corinth made a united attack on Paul and brought him to the place of judgment. "This man," they charged, "is persuading the people to worship God in ways contrary to the law."

Just as Paul was about to speak, Gallio said to them, "If you Jews were making a complaint about some misdemeanor or serious crime, it would be reasonable for me to listen to you. But since it involves questions about words and names and your own law—settle the matter yourselves. I will not be a judge of such things." So he drove them off. Then the crowd there turned on Sosthenes the synagogue leader and beat him in front of the proconsul; and Gallio showed no concern whatever.

PRISCILLA, AQUILA AND APOLLOS

Paul stayed on in Corinth for some time. Then he left the brothers and sisters and sailed for Syria, accompanied by Priscilla and Aquila. Before he sailed, he had his hair cut off at Cenchreae because of a vow he had taken. They arrived at Ephesus, where Paul left Priscilla and Aquila. He himself went into the synagogue and reasoned with the Jews. When they asked him to spend more time with them, he declined. But as he left, he promised, "I will come back if it is God's will." Then he set sail from Ephesus. When he landed at Caesarea, he went up to Jerusalem and greeted the church and then went down to Antioch.

After spending some time in Antioch, Paul set out from there and traveled from place to place throughout the region of Galatia and Phrygia, strengthening all the disciples.

Meanwhile a Jew named Apollos, a native of Alexandria, came to Ephesus. He was a learned man, with a thorough knowledge of the Scriptures. He had been instructed in the way of the Lord, and he spoke with great fervor and taught about Jesus accurately, though he knew only the baptism of John. He began to speak boldly in the synagogue. When Priscilla and Aquila heard him, they invited him to their home and explained to him the way of God more adequately.

When Apollos wanted to go to Achaia, the brothers and sisters encouraged him and wrote to the disciples there to welcome him. When he arrived, he was a great help to those who by grace had believed. For he vigorously refuted his Jewish opponents in public debate,

proving from the Scriptures that Jesus was the Messiah . . .

ROMANS 16:1–5

I commend to you our sister Phoebe, a deacon of the church in Cenchreae. I ask you to receive her in the Lord in a way worthy of His people and to give her any help she may need from you, for she has been the benefactor of many people, including me.

Greet Priscilla and Aquila, my co-workers in Christ Jesus. They risked their lives for me. Not only I but all the churches of the Gentiles are grateful to them.

Greet also the church that meets at their house . . . .

I CORINTHIANS 16:19

The churches in the province of Asia send you greetings. Aquila and Priscilla greet you warmly in the Lord, and so does the church that meets at their house.

There tends to be a name that rings louder in a lot of stories we read, maybe one person that is given more of a leadership role or the mouthpiece, and we paint them as the hero of the story. However, much like our lives, there are always many people behind the curtain who have helped us get to where we are, providing what we need to make the journey God asks of us.

I think about my own experience with my small business, Cleerely Stated, and looking back, it is truly miraculous the way God connected dots and provided the people I have needed every step of the way. While my name may be on the cover of the devotional guide you are currently reading, there are a thousand names that are responsible for making this opportunity a reality.

Reading about Paul's journey in the Scriptures above, we see the names of those who were present, and those are just the ones that are mentioned. In particular, I am drawn to Priscilla and Aquila, a couple who mentored Paul and helped him grow in his understanding of Jesus. Mentioned in Acts, Romans, and 1 Corinthians, they make it apparent that Paul was aware that teamwork was the only way to make the dream work. We were never meant to be stand-alone preachers, receiving credit for our revelations; rather, we are all meant to labor together, giving God the credit as we spread His kingdom far and wide.

We are all meant to labor together, giving God the credit as we spread His kingdom far and wide.

1. *Scripture tells us that the Lord spoke to Paul in a vision one night and said, "Do not be afraid; keep on speaking, do not be silent." What do you think Paul was afraid of?*

2. *Paul obviously had people he could have settled down with in many areas, but he remained on mission for God. What do you believe this looks like in your own life—to not settle or remain stagnant?*

3. The eyes and the mouth are visible and easy to recognize. What roles do you associate with those parts of the body of Christ and what parts feel more hidden? Which do you tend to play?

4. Romans says that Pricilla and Aquila risked their lives for Paul so that he could continue with his ministry. What sacrifices have people in your life made so that you could show up in the space you needed to?

5. Teamwork implies that we have to be willing to give help and receive it. What do you think you're better at? How can you be a better team player?

Dear Lord, thank You for these passages of Scripture that reveal to me so much about how Paul viewed the people of God that surrounded him. Even when he was the one preaching or leading, he was aware that it was those that surrounded him, taught him, encouraged him, housed him, helped him, and loved him that allowed him to do what he did for You. Will You help me walk in that same humility and honor?

Help me keep my eyes straight ahead, not looking to the right or the left or desiring a different role than the one I am given. I know that if You assign it, significance is already present. Just like Priscilla and Aquila, help me show up well so that I can take part in the great things You have stored up for those who love You.

Thank You for showing me the power of teamwork. It is the system of the Kingdom, just as we are the body of Christ. Each person plays a different part and all come together to point to You.

Maximize the value I put on my assignments, taking them to heart and giving all that I have wherever You call me. I praise You for this place—this ground, this plow, this fruit, this life. All is a gift from You.

I will speak to the beauty, purpose, and kindness that others extend and welcome their offerings, knowing that our contributions are seen and loved by You.

In the collaborative, generous, and sovereign name of Jesus, amen.

MEDITATE ON HIS LOVE

ECCLESIASTES 4:9–12 ESV

Two are better than one, because they have a good reward for their toil. For if they fall, one will lift up his fellow. But woe to him who is alone when he falls and has not another to lift him up! Again, if two lie together, they keep warm, but how can one keep warm alone? And though a man might prevail against one who is alone, two will withstand him—a threefold cord is not quickly broken.

PROVERBS 27:17 ESV

Iron sharpens iron, and one man sharpens another.

EPHESIANS 4:16 ESV

From whom the whole body, joined and held together by every joint with which it is equipped, *when each part is working properly, makes the body grow so that it builds itself up in love.*

HEBREWS 10:24–25 ESV

And let us consider how to stir up one another to love and good works, not neglecting to meet together, as is the habit of some, but encouraging one another, and all the more as you see the Day drawing near.

I CORINTHIANS 12:14–16 ESV

For the body does not consist of one member but of many. If the foot should say, "Because I am not a hand, I do not belong to the body," that would not make it any less a part of the body. And if the ear should say, "Because I am not an eye, I do not belong to the body," that would not make it any less a part of the body.

LEARN ABOUT HIS LOVE

Motivated by Unity

MARK 3:20-35; MATTHEW 12:22-37 NIV

Then Jesus entered a house, and again a crowd gathered, so that He and His disciples were not even able to eat. When His family heard about this, they went to take charge of Him, for they said, "He is out of His mind." And the teachers of the law who came down from Jerusalem said, "He is possessed by Beelzebul! By the prince of demons He is driving out demons."

So Jesus called them over to Him and began to speak to them in parables: "How can Satan drive out Satan? If a kingdom is divided against itself, that kingdom cannot stand. If a house is divided against itself, that house cannot stand. And if Satan opposes himself and is divided, he cannot stand; his end has come. In fact, no one can enter a strong man's house without first tying him up. Then he can plunder the strong man's house. Truly I tell you, people can be forgiven all their sins and every slander they utter, but whoever blasphemes against the Holy Spirit will never be forgiven; they are guilty of an eternal sin."

He said this because they were saying, "He has an impure spirit."

Then Jesus' mother and brothers arrived. Standing outside, they sent someone in to call Him. A crowd was sitting around Him, and they told Him, "Your mother and brothers are outside looking for You."

"Who are my mother and my brothers?" He asked.

Then He looked at those seated in a circle around Him and said, "Here are my mother and my brothers! Whoever does God's will is my brother and sister and mother." . . .

MATTHEW 12:22-37

Then they brought Him a demon-possessed man who was blind and mute, and Jesus healed him, so that he could both talk and see. All the people were astonished and said, "Could this be the Son of David?"

But when the Pharisees heard this, they said, "It is only by Beelzebul, the prince of demons, that this fellow drives out demons."

Jesus knew their thoughts and said to them, "Every kingdom divided against itself will be ruined, and every city or household divided *against itself will not stand. If Satan drives out Satan, he is divided against himself. How then can his kingdom stand? And if I drive out demons by Beelzebul, by whom do your people drive them out? So then, they will be your judges. But if it is by the Spirit of God that I drive out demons, then the kingdom of God has come upon you.*

"Or again, how can anyone enter a strong man's house and carry off his possessions unless he first ties up the strong man? Then he can plunder his house.

"Whoever is not with me is against me, and whoever does not gather with me scatters. And so I tell you, every kind of sin and slander can be forgiven, but blasphemy against the Spirit will not be forgiven. Anyone who speaks a word against the Son of Man will be forgiven, but anyone who speaks against the Holy Spirit will not be forgiven, either in this age or in the age to come.

"Make a tree good and its fruit will be good, or make a tree bad and its fruit will be bad, for a tree is recognized by its fruit. You brood of vipers, how can you who are evil say anything good? For the mouth speaks what the heart is full of. A good man brings good things out of the good stored up in him, and an evil man brings evil things out of the evil stored up in him. But I tell you that everyone will have to give account on the day of judgment for every empty word they have spoken. For by your words you will be acquitted, and by your words you will be condemned."

In news headlines, social media, advertisements, and all throughout culture, unity is a hot topic. We hashtag it, get behind the movement when it's trending, and voice our desire for change. However, lately I have really been asking my own heart, *If Jesus were here in the flesh, what would He say? Where would His time be directed? What would He say to make a true difference?*

I think we get a good showing of where His heart would land based on this Scripture. When Jesus says, "If a house is divided against itself, it cannot stand," the word "house" comes from the Greek New Testament term *oikos*, which translates better to the English word "family." The Pharisees were concerned with persuading everyone that this demon-possessed man could only be healed by the prince of demons, thereby condemning Jesus and slandering His identity. Because of this, the Pharisees missed out on the entire miracle of this man's healing. Their hardened hearts were revealed, showing that they really didn't understand the power of Jesus, despite all they knew. Because if so, wouldn't they have wanted healing for this man? Wouldn't they trust that if Jesus brought it to pass, it was good and trustworthy?

Jesus didn't care about labels, backgrounds, or past experiences. After all, He is the maker of them all! His concern was that those around Him would desire to do the will of His father; that is what made them family. Is that how we define unity? And much like Jesus, do we desire hope, healing, and holiness for all people or just those we prefer or understand?

Jesus already defined unity; it is not ours to redefine. Once we can actually grasp the power of His truth and love in action, we will fight for all our family, familiar or not.

> Jesus didn't care about labels, backgrounds, or past experiences. After all, He is the maker of them all!

PONDER HIS LOVE

1. *When it comes to unity, what do you tend to think about? What do you think this Scripture reveals about your definition? Do you feel like you've grown more in this area with the recent cultural changes?*

2. *What are some ways you struggle to put Jesus before every other loyalty? Why do you think that is and how can you work to put Him first?*

3. *Jesus talks about the power of words and how we will one day stand before the judgment seat for all that we have said. Does this make you fearful? Do you believe your words sow life or death into yourself and those around you?*

4. *When Jesus said, "Who are my mother and my brothers?" He was insinuating that His true family is anyone who does the will of His Father. How do you see family?*

5. *In a very practical sense, how can you better apply this definition of unity and protection of God's people in your own life? What could you change or implement that would build others up in Him?*

Dear Lord, thank You for this story that challenges and inspires my heart to see, think, and respond differently. Reading this miracle, I wonder how many times I have been like the Pharisees, eager to point out the reason someone doesn't deserve Your truth and grace. I'm sorry for ever letting my constructed idea of Your truth supersede what is truly Your heart.

Open my eyes to Your definition of unity, justice, and mercy. Examine my heart and show me any places that reveal prejudices, fear, scarcity, or judgment. My mission on this earth is to extend Your family, not divide it. Help me give all my energy and resources to building a stronger foundation for You rather than proving a point, pointing out the stones in other's eyes, or protecting my self-righteous definition based on my comfort zone.

Thank You for accepting me fully and offering me the position that defines every other position in my life: child of the King. Your mercy is endless, and Your faithfulness, despite my doubt, humbles my heart.

Forge in me a protective nature of all Your people, near and far. What You unify, no man can separate or destroy. Thank You for giving me the power of the Holy Spirit inside of me so that I can deny my flesh and choose what matters forever with You.

Help me be a place of good ground—a tree with fruit that bears Your name and blesses Your people. Show me how to fill my heart with good things so it overflows onto myself and others, reflecting who You are and how You see.

In the unifying, majestic, and authoritative name of Jesus, amen.

MEDITATE ON HIS LOVE

I CORINTHIANS 1:10 NIV

I appeal to you, brothers and sisters, in the name of our Lord Jesus Christ, that all of you agree with one another in what you say and that there be no divisions among you, but that you be perfectly united in mind and thought.

ACTS 4:32 NIV

All the believers were one in heart and mind. No one claimed that any of their possessions was their own, but they shared everything they had.

GALATIANS 3:28 NIV

There is neither Jew nor Gentile, neither slave nor free, nor is there male and female, for you are all one in Christ Jesus.

ROMANS 14:19 NIV

Let us therefore make every effort to do what leads to peace and to mutual edification.

JOHN 17:23 NIV

I in them and you in Me—so that they may be brought to complete unity. Then the world will know that you sent Me and have loved them even as you have loved Me.

LEARN ABOUT HIS LOVE

Rested to Refresh

EXODUS 20:1-11 NIV; MARK 2:23-28; HEBREWS 4:1-13 NLT

THE TEN COMMANDMENTS

And God spoke all these words: "I am the Lord *your God, who brought you out of Egypt, out of the land of slavery.*

"You shall have no other gods before me.

"You shall not make for yourself an image in the form of anything in heaven above or on the earth beneath or in the waters below. You shall not bow down to them or worship them; for I, the Lord *your God, am a jealous God, punishing the children for the sin of the parents to the third and fourth generation of those who hate me, but showing love to a thousand generations of those who love me and keep my commandments.*

"You shall not misuse the name of the Lord *your God, for the* Lord *will not hold anyone guiltless who misuses his name.*

"Remember the Sabbath day by keeping it holy. Six days you shall labor and do all your work, but the seventh day is a sabbath to the Lord *your God. On it you shall not do any work, neither you, nor your son or daughter, nor your male or female servant, nor your animals, nor any foreigner residing in your towns. For in six days the* Lord *made the heavens and the earth, the sea, and all that is in them, but he rested on the seventh day. Therefore the* Lord *blessed the Sabbath day and made it holy.*

"Honor your father and your mother, so that you may live long in the land the Lord *your God is giving you.*

"You shall not murder.

"You shall not commit adultery.

"You shall not steal.

"You shall not give false testimony against your neighbor.

"You shall not covet your neighbor's house. You shall not covet your neighbor's wife, or his male or female servant, his ox or donkey, or anything that belongs to your neighbor."...

One Sabbath day as Jesus was walking through some grainfields, His disciples began breaking off heads of grain to eat. But the Pharisees said to Jesus, "Look, why are they breaking the law by harvesting grain on the Sabbath?"

Jesus said to them, "Haven't you ever read in the Scriptures what David did when he and his companions were hungry? He went into the house of God (during the days when Abiathar was high priest) and broke the law by eating the sacred loaves of bread that only the priests are allowed to eat. He also gave some to his companions."

Then Jesus said to them, "The Sabbath was made to meet the needs of people, and not people to meet the requirements of the Sabbath. So the Son of Man is Lord, even over the Sabbath!" . . .

HEBREWS 4:1-13

PROMISED REST FOR GOD'S PEOPLE

God's promise of entering His rest still stands, so we ought to tremble with fear that some of you might fail to experience it. For this good news—that God has prepared this rest—has been announced to us just as it was to them. But it did them no good because they didn't share the faith of those who listened to God. For only we who believe can enter His rest. As for the others, God said,

"In my anger I took an oath:
  'They will never enter my place of rest,'"

even though this rest has been ready since He made the world. We know it is ready because of the place in the Scriptures where it mentions the seventh day: "On the seventh day God rested from all His work." But in the other passage God said, "They will never enter my place of rest."

So God's rest is there for people to enter, but those who first heard this good news failed to enter because they disobeyed God. So God set another time for entering his rest, and that time is today. God announced this through David much later in the words already quoted:

"Today when you hear his voice,
  don't harden your hearts."

Now if Joshua had succeeded in giving them this rest, God would not have spoken about another day of rest still to come. So there is a special rest still waiting for the people of God. For all who have entered into God's rest have rested from their labors, just as God did after creating the world. So let us do our best to enter that rest. But if we disobey God, as the people of Israel did, we will fall.

For the word of God is alive and powerful. It is sharper than the sharpest two-edged sword, cutting between soul and spirit, between joint and marrow. It exposes our innermost thoughts and desires. Nothing in all creation is hidden from God. Everything is naked and exposed before His eyes, and He is the one to whom we are accountable.

How many of us find that after a vacation, we need a vacation from our vacation? Because upon returning to our usual work routines and everyday activities, we are still exhausted, overwhelmed, and stressed to the hilt. Recently studying about the Sabbath, I loved how Mark tells us that the Sabbath was created by God to meet the needs of the people, not for people to meet the requirements of the Sabbath. There is a striking difference. It also shows us that when God instructed us to rest, it was never about finding a hammock and a good book, although that is perfectly acceptable; rather, it is about us operating from a posture of rest in every moment of our lives.

We cannot be people that refresh others in God's Spirit when our own lives are at capacity and without margin. When Hebrews tells us to "do our best to enter that rest," it is reminding us that if we hold tight to this elusive definition of rest as a sedentary position, we will miss out on the promise God has already given us when He fulfilled the law.

This is why the tradition of the Sabbath was always so important for the Jewish people—the reminder that no matter the workload, our shoulders must take a breather. The beautiful part about this for us is that when Jesus came, He allowed us to release every burden onto Him, and not just on the Sabbath. Rest isn't to be earned; it is a gift—one that is meant to be opened, enjoyed, and accessed at all moments because we know who is in charge.

As we sit with Him, soak in His presence, and savor His Word, we allow our souls to be satisfied in Him. We stop all our striving, no longer feeling the need to perform, and we become responders to this deep rest we have been given. What a gift—to know that the Good Shepherd can still our souls and quiet our hearts, no matter the waves that crash in our lives. Rest is no longer a reaction to a solution but a lifestyle cultivated through learning our Savior's heart.

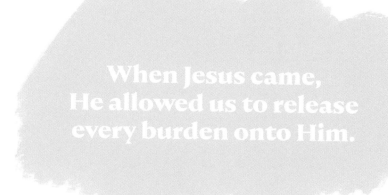

When Jesus came,
He allowed us to release
every burden onto Him.

1. *How do you define rest in your current life? Does it align with the Word and the promise of the rest of Jesus?*

2. *Do you practice the Sabbath? If so, how? If not, how could you be more intentional with it?*

3. *Do you believe you operate from a posture of rest? If not, why? What tends to trigger you into striving, worrying, and overworking your body, mind, heart, or soul?*

4. *What do you think would happen in your life if you took these Scriptures seriously? What might shift?*

5. *Hebrews says divine wisdom is the entrance to this place of rest. However, it does not mention knowledge. What is the difference? Do you think we sometimes confuse trusting His Word with knowing the outcome?*

Dear Lord, my soul reads these Scriptures and I find the deep breath I have been searching for all day. Thank You for this. How is it that the God of the universe would find me worthy enough to take everything off my shoulders and place it on His? It is the greatest mystery and blessing of my life.

Will You help me surrender my agenda and everything on it? You are the keeper of time, the giver of all good gifts, and the holder of all things holy. You can do anything all of the sudden; there is no need for me to strive.

Show me how to operate from a posture of rest. Will You help me redefine the word "rest" in my life, stripping away all preconceived notions and definitions that do not align with Your Word? Counsel me in how to show up in each area of my life, while keeping my boundary lines in pleasant places. Remove my fear of deadlines, unmet expectations, and inadequacy as I lean into the rest that You have already provided for my soul and my life.

As I declare this new stance in my life, help me not be surprised when life brushes up against it, doing its best to convince me to worry, toil, fear, or be consumed with what I see. Lead me back to Your Word and hide me in the shadow of Your wings.

My ache is for heaven so my rest is sure on this earth. Thank You, Father.

In the peaceful, restful, and sovereign name of Jesus, amen.

MEDITATE ON HIS LOVE

PSALM 62:1 NIV

Truly my soul finds rest in God; my salvation comes from Him.

PSALM 116:7 ESV

Return, O my soul, to your rest; for the LORD has dealt bountifully with you.

MATTHEW 11:29–30 ESV

Take my yoke upon you and learn from me, for I am gentle and humble in heart, and you will find rest for your souls. For my yoke is easy and my burden is light.

PROVERBS 19:23 ESV

The fear of the LORD leads to life, and whoever has it rests satisfied; he will not be visited by harm.

EXODUS 33:14 ESV

And he said, "My presence will go with you, and I will give you rest."

LEARN ABOUT HIS LOVE

What Love Really Means

I CORINTHIANS 13; 1 JOHN 3:10–24 NIV

If I speak in the tongues of men or of angels, but do not have love, I am only a resounding gong or a clanging cymbal. If I have the gift of prophecy and can fathom all mysteries and all knowledge, and if I have a faith that can move mountains, but do not have love, I am nothing. If I give all I possess to the poor and give over my body to hardship that I may boast, but do not have love, I gain nothing.

Love is patient, love is kind. It does not envy, it does not boast, it is not proud. It does not dishonor others, it is not self-seeking, it is not easily angered, it keeps no record of wrongs. Love does not delight in evil but rejoices with the truth. It always protects, always trusts, always hopes, always perseveres.

Love never fails. But where there are prophecies, they will cease; where there are tongues, they will be stilled; where there is knowledge, it will pass away. For we know in part and we prophesy in part, but when completeness comes, what is in part disappears. When I was a child, I talked like a child, I thought like a child, I reasoned like a child. When I became a man, I put the ways of childhood behind me. For now we see only a reflection as in a mirror; then we shall see face to face. Now I know in part; then I shall know fully, even as I am fully known.

And now these three remain: faith, hope and love. But the greatest of these is love . . . .

I JOHN 3:10–24

This is how we know who the children of God are and who the children of the devil are: Anyone who does not do what is right is not God's child, nor is anyone who does not love their brother and sister.

MORE ON LOVE AND HATRED

For this is the message you heard from the beginning: We should love one another. Do not be like Cain, who belonged to the evil one and murdered his brother. And why did he murder him? Because his own actions were evil and his brother's were righteous. Do not be surprised, my brothers and sisters, if the world hates you. We know that we have passed from death to life, because we love each other. Anyone who does not love remains in death. Anyone who hates a brother or sister is a murderer, and you know that no murderer has eternal life residing in him.

This is how we know what love is: Jesus Christ laid down His life for us. And we ought to lay down our lives for our brothers and sisters. If anyone has material possessions and sees a brother or sister in need but has no pity on them, how can the love of God be in that person? Dear children, let us not love with words or speech but with actions and in truth.

This is how we know that we belong to the truth and how we set our hearts at rest in His presence: If our hearts condemn us, we know that God is greater than our hearts, and He knows everything. Dear friends, if our hearts do not condemn us, we have confidence before God and receive from Him anything we ask, because we keep His commands and do what pleases Him. And this is His command: to believe in the name of His Son, Jesus Christ, and to love one another as He commanded us. The one who keeps God's commands lives in Him, and He in them. And this is how we know that He lives in us: We know it by the Spirit He gave us.

How can we be love in action if we don't know what love really means? We might have heard I Corinthians 13 at a wedding or at church when someone was preaching about love, allowing us to somewhat close our ears to what God is really saying because we have heard it before. However, I challenged myself to imagine God saying it to me personally, as if I were standing right in front of Him. The intimacy was almost too much as I allowed the truth of His love to wash over my soul.

Because, you see, we often make our own definitions of biblical principles based on our ability to walk them out. Our understanding of such words is limited by the reality of our own humanity and circumstances, not allowing us to really grasp what they mean for our lives. When I closed my eyes and allowed myself to imagine the King of kings reading this to me, I realized that He was wanting me to understand how He loves me, and therefore, how He loves you!

This is the power that we have as His children—to love Him, ourselves, and others in return. Though we will spend our lives falling short, His Spirit will help us, empower us, and move us to act in ways that only the Spirit can. First John 19 says that this is "how we set our hearts at rest in His presence."

Our striving may cease; our job is simply to love whomever He brings to us, in whatever capacity He asks, wherever we are. There is no greater calling.

Though we will spend our lives falling short, His Spirit will help us, empower us, and move us to act in ways that only the Spirit can.

PONDER HIS LOVE

1. *When reading through the qualities of love in I Corinthians, what do you believe is easiest for you? Hardest? Why do you think that is?*

2. *These passages talk about the importance of expressing love in action. However, they also discuss the danger of acting without love. What does this mean?*

3. *The Scriptures from 1 John really dive into the necessity of loving one another if we are to be called children of God. When you give love to others, how do you filter it through your preferences and favoritism?*

4. *What are some ways you have viewed love in the past (or currently) that are childish and don't align with these Scriptures? How can you renew your mind with truth?*

5. *Do you struggle to believe that God could really love you this way? Why?*

Dear Lord, reading these reminders of what love truly means makes my heart soar and my spirit so grateful. Thank You for being the perfect example of every word that You speak. Your love knows no bounds, recklessly pursuing every part of my heart.

Will You help me redefine love in my own life? Break down any boxes based on the world's definition of love, and remove any barriers based on past hurts I have experienced. Illuminate this word in a new way—Your way—so that I can be love in action in every place You position me. Help me be a constant reflection of Your sacrifice, the ultimate demonstration of love on the cross.

As I continue forward, in every season of my life, will You equip me to love well? I know that when I serve others and prioritize You, my own heart is refreshed. You are the living water, the well that doesn't run dry, and You fill me to overflowing.

Help me sit and be with You so that I can experience Your love. Affirm my place at Your feet and as Your child; I praise You for all that You are and all that You've done for me. I commit to spending my life demonstrating such love to those around me, knowing that when I fall short, You will cover my way.

Love that practices patience and kindness, serves others, keeps no record of wrongs, and always trusts, protects, and perseveres—that's what I long to give and receive.

In the unwavering, unconditional, and relentless love of Jesus, amen.

MEDITATE ON HIS LOVE

COLOSSIANS 3:14 ESV

And above all these put on love, which binds everything together in perfect harmony.

I PETER 1:22 ESV

Having purified your souls by your obedience to the truth for a sincere brotherly love, love one another earnestly from a pure heart.

LUKE 6:35 ESV

But love your enemies, and do good, and lend, expecting nothing in return, and your reward will be great, and you will be sons of the Most High, for he is kind to the ungrateful and the evil.

ROMANS 12:9 ESV

Let love be genuine. Abhor what is evil; hold fast to what is good.

PROVERBS 3:3-4 ESV

Let not steadfast love and faithfulness forsake you; bind them around your neck; write them on the tablet of your heart. So you will find favor and good success in the sight of God and man.

For more on this topic, scan the QR code for a video message from Cleere.

Want more from Cleere?

You can find her devotionals and
Prayers to Share on dayspring.com,
as well as several retail stores near you.

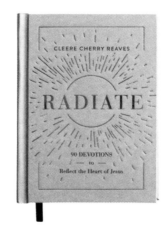

ABOUT THE AUTHOR

Cleere Cherry Reaves

CLEERE CHERRY REAVES is the owner and creator of *Cleerely Stated*, a successful business that started with a simple blog and turned into a full product line that can be found online and in retail stores all over the United States. Well-known for her easy-to-relate-to, practical writing style, Cleere's mission is to help others see themselves and the world around them through the eyes of Jesus. Cleere now hosts a growing podcast called *Let's Be Cleere*, where she hopes people are encouraged by the raw, real love of Jesus. She was born and raised in Greenville, North Carolina. She's a proud alumnus of the University of North Carolina at Chapel Hill and loves to live life to the fullest.

LIVE YOUR FAITH

Dear Friend,

This Bible resource was prayerfully crafted with you in mind—it was thoughtfully written, designed, and packaged to encourage you right where you are. At DaySpring Bibles, our vision is to see every person experience the life-changing message of God's love, not just on Sundays, but every day of the week. As we worked through rough drafts, design changes, edits and details, we prayed for you to encounter His unfailing love and indescribable peace within the pages of this book. It is our hope that this resource doesn't only fill your head with knowledge, but strengthens your connection with and understanding of God.

THE DAYSPRING BIBLE TEAM

Additional copies of this book and
other DaySpring titles can be purchased
at fine retailers everywhere.
Order online at <u>dayspring.com</u>
or
by phone at 1-877-751-4347